BIRD SOUNDS

Ann Arbor
Science
Library

Bird Sounds

by Gerhard A. Thielcke

ANN ARBOR
THE UNIVERSITY OF MICHIGAN PRESS

Preface

Familiarity with bird sounds is the basic tool of every ornithologist who deals with birds in the wild. But their vocalizations are also fruitful objects of research for scientists in many other disciplines. The anatomist is interested in the sound-producing organs and the ear. The physiologist studies the processes of sound production and sound perception. The behavioral researcher is interested in how birds react to sounds, and the student of evolution tries to determine the role of vocabulary in the formation of species.

We could go on with this list indefinitely, but even this brief enumeration suggests the many points of contact between bioacoustics and other branches of scientific research. It is not the least of the reasons why we are attracted to study animal sounds. In this book I have dealt in detail with the importance of bird sounds as a means of communication and a factor in evolution because it is these areas, in particular, that have offered very promising take-off points for fresh studies.

As I write these lines, a great tit is chiming its song outside my window, a house sparrow scolds in front of its nest under the roof, and a male blackbird is singing softly in a nearby bush. Their sounds are still music in my ears, as they were long ago before I knew anything about the sound spectrograph, the origin of species, and behavioral research. I say this in order to give some assurance to the reader who may be afraid he will lose his love of nature if he reads any further.

GERHARD THIELCKE

Contents

I. *Bird Sounds in Black and White*

If we want to know exactly how the movements of an animal take place, we film them and then observe them in slow motion; but even that is not enough for the behavioral researcher who would like to get an even more exact grasp of the process. So he compares the successive film shots and takes measurements. To make the results of his labors clear and graphic, he arranges the individual pictures alongside each other so that the observer *sees* the animal's movement (Fig. 1 a).

A similar procedure can be used for vocal sounds (vocalizations). We record them on tape and play them back at slow speed. Using a tape recorder, however, we cannot hold the same pitch and change only the speed. Altering the speed of the tape means distorting the pitch. Quite apart from that fact, playback at reduced speed brings us no further in the realm of hearing than slow-motion pictures do in the realm of seeing. What we want is to have the sounds in black and white so that we can analyze them in precise detail. Today we can do this with the help of sound spectrograms, i.e., pictures taken by a sound spectrograph. The instrument is also called a sonagraph, and the pictures sonagrams.

To familiarize the reader with sound spectrograms, I have chosen the 'hooting' of the tawny owl as my example (Fig. 1 b, c). Most readers will be familiar with the sound in question. The sound spectrogram is to be read from left to right. The time is recorded on the base line. The owl's

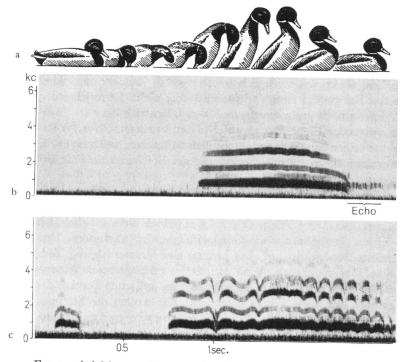

Fig. 1. (*a*) Movement pattern of mallard at mating time; drawing based on films by H. Kacher in von de Wall, 1963. (*b*) and (*c*) sound pattern of tawny owl in two strophes.

'tone', which sounds like *huuu,* is horizontal (Fig. 1 b), hence it is not broken up in time. It lasts 0.85 seconds. After a pause of several seconds, there is a very short 'tone' lasting less than 0.15 seconds. It heralds a long 'tone' that is held for almost 1.2 seconds (Fig. 1 c). These three 'tones' are the song of the tawny owl.

The sound spectrogram tells us something more than just the number of tones and their duration. It also informs us about their pitch. We can read this on the vertical scale (at the left) which ranges from 0–6 kc (kilocycles). From physics we know that 1 kilocycle equals 1000 cycles (vibrations) per second. The faster the air particles vibrate, the higher we perceive the tone to be. And the higher the tone is, the farther it departs from the base line. The *huuu* sound in figure 1 b rises somewhat in pitch and then drops somewhat again at the end. The pitch of the long 'tone' in figure 1 c fluctuates in quick succession. We hear this as *hu^{u}u^{u}u^{u}u^{u}u*.

Now usually there is no question of tones when we are dealing with animal sounds, because a tone in physics consists of only one single frequency. In musicology, as opposed to physics, a tone is regarded as the mixture of fundamental tone and overtones that occurs when we strike a piano key for example. But even musicologists would not agree with us if we were to label the individual components of a bird song as tones. For bird sounds, in contrast to many instrument tones, are almost always discordant combinations that fluctuate in pitch. Such sound mixtures are called noises.

It would be asking too much of the reader if I were to describe the song of the nightingale as a series of noises. So here I use the term 'elements' for the components of a strophe that are separated by pauses. In our example, two elements are combined to form one strophe in figure 1 c. The pauses before the next strophe, which would look like figure 1 b again, are greater than those between the elements. The strophe in figure 1 b consists of only one element. Several strophes are called a 'song'. In our terminology here, the tawny owl *sings* just as surely as the blackbird does, because the significance of the sounds of both species is the same.

Now that we know how to read duration and pitch off a spectrogram, we must concern ourselves with the loudness or volume of the sound. Whereas pitch is altered by variations in the speed with which the air particles vibrate, loudness is determined by the degree of contact and collision between the air particles. On a sound spectrogram very loud tones show up as very black, broad bands. Very soft tones show up as gray and slender bands. There is a whole range of gradual shading between these two extremes, but the width of the band allows us to draw some conclusion about the loudness of the sound only if the pitch remains practically unchanged. For the sharper the rise or drop in pitch, the more slender the band becomes.

Each element of the song of the tawny owl is composed of pitch bands that overlay one another and that vary in loudness. Together they give the timbre that is characteristic of this sound. The overtones of many bird sounds are so soft that the sound spectrograph does not record them. Hence they are missing in many of the illustrations that follow.

Whether we are observing a mating mallard or eavesdropping on a singing tawny owl, we always see only a fraction of the animal's behavior. Once the performance is over, we are thrown back completely on our own memory if we want to reconstruct the process. With the graphic record of film or spectrogram, however, we can observe and compare movement or tone over and over again. That is the great advantage of this procedure.

We should also point out what we cannot do with spectrograms. Even the expert reader of sound spectrograms will be able to get only an approximate idea of the sound from the spectrogram itself. Pictures and diagrams alone will not give someone a knowledgeable acquaintance with bird sounds.

The aim of this book is to familiarize the reader with the biology of vocalizations. He cannot gain such familiarity if he does not grasp the underlying principle of the sound spectrogram. So we shall retrace our steps a bit, describing how people represented bird sounds in the past and illustrating the interpretation of sound spectrograms with a second example.

From March to July every stroller can hear a particular bird around the edge of the woods. It is the yellowhammer, repeating its simple strophe over and over again. Before the age of tape recorders and sound spectrograms, people set bird sounds to music or transcribed them in words. The strophe of the yellowhammer, for example, might be transcribed as: "see, see, see, see, see, see, see, up in the tree" (Fig. 2 a). One tried to approximate the rhythm and timbre of the yellowhammer's sound as much as possible, and the little sentence helped the neophyte student of bird calls to recognize it. But that is about all the help it offered.

At first glance the sound spectrogram of the yellowhammer's song may bewilder the reader with its many details. On the other hand, it does show clearly that the bird first repeats the same sound-pattern ten times, and then closes its strophe with another long drawn-out element. When one cannot tell for sure whether there is a pause between two elements, they are called a 'compound element'. Thus the strophe of the yellowhammer depicted here consists of ten compound elements (from 'see' to 'the') and one closing element ('tree'). Each separate compound element is very short, lasting only a bit more than 0.1 second. We do not perceive the temporal partition in the compound element because our ear is too 'dull' to pick it up. The yellowhammer is capable of hearing the dichotomy because birds can discern more acoustic details in a given time than we can. If *we* want to hear the partition, we must play back the song at a slower speed on our tape recorder.

Whereas the elements of the tawny owl's song are made up of single, superposed frequency-bands, the ten compound elements of the yellowhammer's strophe are composed of many closely meshed frequency-bands with con-

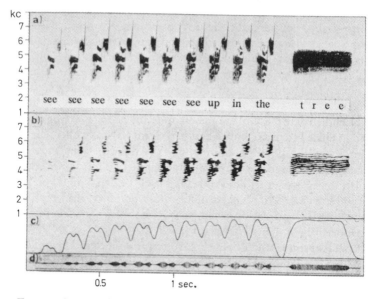

FIG. 2. Same yellowhammer strophe: (*a*) sound spectrogram, WIDE setting, (*b*) sound spectrogram, NARROW setting, (*c*) intensity graph, (*d*) oscillogram.

siderable jumps in tone. At the end of each compound element the pitch rises markedly. The frequency-bands of the last element lie so closely over one another that they merge in our illustration.

Sound spectrograms can be made in two different ways. With the setting WIDE (Fig. 2 a) we get clearer pictures that are better delimited in terms of time. The setting NARROW (Fig. 2 b) shows us the pitch more accurately. If we make a copy of the spectrogram from the original, as has often been the case here, we usually lose the fine details of density. But we can get an approximate reading of the loudness cycle because very soft segments are delineated only very weakly if at all. Thus the incompleteness of the first compound element in our spectrogram leads us to conclude that the yellowhammer begins its strophe softly and then gets louder. The loudness graph (Fig. 2 c) confirms this conjecture. It shows that the compound elements start off jerkily and then become continuously louder; and that the closing element is just about as loud as the tenth element ('the') is. But there is something else to be gleaned from this graph. It shows that the concluding element maintains the same volume whereas the second part of the compound element is softer than the first.

Now that we have familiarized ourselves with the strophe of the yellowhammer in a sound spectrogram (Fig. 2 a, b) and in an intensity graph (Fig. 2 c), we will take a look at it in an oscillogram (Fig. 2 d). Again we read the duration of the sound from the base line. The louder the sound is, the farther it moves out on either side of the base line. The pitch cannot be read off directly; it must be calculated on the basis of the distance between the single impulses. The faster they follow each other, the higher is the tone.

Oscillograms and sound spectrograms will be encountered over and over again in treatments of animal sounds. Therefore, we shall compare and contrast the two methods of representation once more in a schematic way (Fig. 3). First we see a tone with a steady pitch of 200 cycles (Fig. 3 a). This means that a particle of air oscillates back and forth 200 times per second, or 20 times in 1/10 of a second. A particle of air oscillates continuously around the same point. It would be senseless to depict this directly, for we would get nothing but a line. But if we draw a horizontal line with a time scale and record the diverging distance of the vertically oscillating air particle from left to right, then we get an oscillogram. The only thing to remember is that we do this with an oscillograph rather than with a crayon. When the wave line cuts the horizontal axis, then the air particle is at its starting point. The points farthest removed from the horizontal axis are the end points of its motion. Rest points and end points together give us the wave line. In the sound spectrogram a tone of the same pitch and loudness shows up as a horizontal bar of equal density throughout.

In figure 3 b the pitch remains unchanged at 200 kilocycles while the loudness is modulated 20 cycles. In 1/20 of a second the tone rises and drops once. In our example that comes to about a 50 percent difference, for at the loudest points the modulation curve is just about twice as far from the horizontal line as it is at the softest points. In the spectrogram we can only ascertain relative loudness; the bar becomes lighter at the soft points and darker at the loud points.

In figure 3 c the tone starts off at 300 cycles. After 1/20 of a second it drops suddenly by 200 cycles and remains there. Accordingly the oscillogram shows 15 vibrations in the first half (1/20 of a second) and 5 vibrations in the second half (1/20 of a second). In the spectrogram the distance from the X-axis decreases with the lower tone.

The pitch in figure 3 d does not remain constant. It fluctuates up and down by 100 cycles, 20 times per second

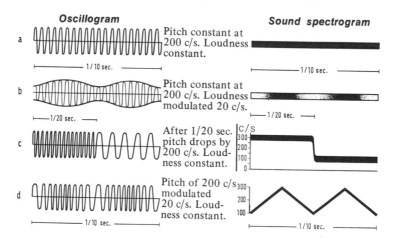

Fig. 3. Four 'tones' depicted schematically as oscillogram and spectrogram.

or 2 times in 1/10 of a second. Those are the two jags in the spectrogram. In the oscillogram we get 20 vibrations. They begin slowly, then become steadily faster and slower by turns. The carrier frequency can be calculated from the vibrations: 20 vibrations in 1/10 of a second come to 200 vibrations per second, i.e., 200 cycles. The pitch pattern here is described technically as follows: the carrier frequency is modulated 20 cycles.

Fluctuations in pitch, such as those depicted in figure 3 d, occur frequently in bird sounds. For this reason I want to mention one possible erroneous interpretation of the spectrograms. In figure 2 it is not clear whether the last element ('tree') consists of a zigzag line such as that in figure 3, or of closely overlaid tone-bands. The WIDE setting (Fig. 2 a) supports the first alternative, the NARROW setting (Fig. 2 b) supports the second alternative. Only the oscillogram can decide here. When we get a picture like that of figure 3 d, then the pitch is modulated and the first possible interpretation is the correct one.

Since sound spectrograms tell us more than any other method of representation, they are the method used most frequently to visualize bird sounds. The case is different with insect sounds, where it is primarily a matter of rhythm and to some extent a matter of loudness as well. Despite the advantages afforded by the clarity of sound spectrograms, I often find that good connoisseurs of bird sounds regard them skeptically. But the reason for this is simply and solely that our aural impressions cause us to picture bird sounds as simpler things than they really are. If we slow down the sounds recorded on our tape, then the result—for all its distortion—is much more comparable to that of a spectrogram. Therefore, we really do hear details which we had assumed to be artifacts of the machine.

II. *Sound Sources*

The ways and means by which animals produce sounds are astonishingly many and varied. Mute swans in rivalry fly close over the water and strike the surface forcefully with their feet. A wood pigeon in its mating flight leaves its song post, mounts upward diagonally with quick beats of its wings, claps its wings together, and then glides downward again. The same process may be repeated until it finally lands on another tree (Fig. 4). The rock dove, the ancestor of our domestic pigeon, draws attention to himself in a similar way at mating time. But he remains at the same altitude instead of mounting upward diagonally (Fig. 4).

The white stork clatters with its beak, both in greeting its partner and challenging rivals (Fig. 5). These clatter strophes, which may be introduced with a hissing sound, do not differ from one another, however, aggressive clatters are accompanied by 'pumping' up and down movements of the wings which are not employed when it greets its partner.

Many birds snap with their beak when they are cornered. But noise comes from the pied flycatcher even before the two halves of its beak touch. Therefore, the sound

10

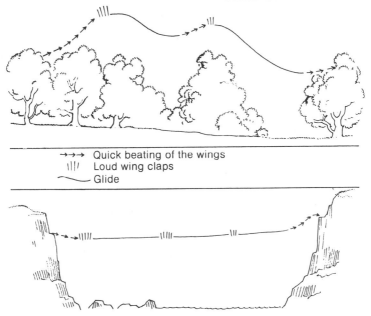

→→→ Quick beating of the wings
‖‖‍ Loud wing claps
⌒ Glide

FIG. 4. Mating flight of the wood pigeon (top) and the rock dove (bottom). (After Goodwin, 1967.)

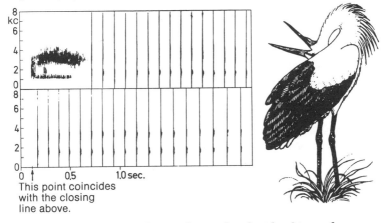

This point coincides
with the closing
line above.

FIG. 5. Clatter of the white stork introduced with a hiss, and one of the positions taken in this process. (Right portion after Bauer and Glutz, 1966.)

source must lie elsewhere, perhaps in the maxillary joint (Curio, 1959). At mating time the manakin, one of the Pipridae, lands with a forceful thrust of his foot and thereby calls attention to himself (Sick, 1959).

Many species must get help from the surrounding air current in order to produce certain noises. Familiar sounds of this sort are the flight noises of ducks, the humming throb of the lapwing, and the bleating of the snipe. The latter sound explains why the snipe is often referred to by some people as the 'sky goat'.

FIG. 6. European woodcock (right) and American woodcock (left). Underneath are their respective wings. The outer primaries of the American woodcock have been converted into sound vibrators. (After Sheldon, 1967.)

These sounds are produced during flight by the agitation of the wings alone, by the elongation or expansion of feathers, e.g., those of the male lapwing, or by specially formed feathers (Fig. 6). The snipe bleats with its outer tail feathers, which can be spread so far away from the adjoining feathers (Fig. 7) that they are set vibrating when the bird plummets downward on a slant. They are reinforced and stiffened at the shaft, and their delicate barbules are notched more firmly. Indeed we find this special structure in the inner vane of the outer rectrice, although the inner vanes are otherwise very soft and weak because they serve as a cushion for the outer vane that lies immediately on top of them. In addition, the inner vane is broadened and the shaft is bent (Fig. 8). The air current that strikes the outer tail feathers of the snipe is interrupted about 11 times per second by the flapping of its wings. Hence the uniform humming tone is split up 11 times (Fig. 7).

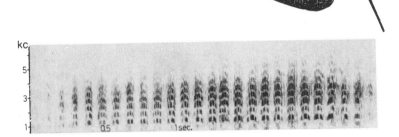

FIG. 7. Bleating of the snipe and the behavior pattern involved. The outer tail feathers are spread apart. When the bird plummets downward at an angle, they are set in vibration. This vibrating motion is interrupted 11 times per second by wing flapping. (Top right portion after Kirby et al.)

Unique in the animal kingdom is the drumming process of woodpeckers. To drum they need an instrument, and so they look for an appropriate one. At brooding time they drum regularly on certain specific spots which can be set vibrating quite easily. An expert can define the species from the acoustic impression of the drum roll alone, because each species has its own drumming pattern.

Fig. 8.   Outer tail feather of the
snipe that vibrates, and average
tail   feather.   The   vibrating
feather has a bent shaft and a
broadened inner vane. (After
Bahr in Stresemann, 1927–34.)

Shaft   Inner vane

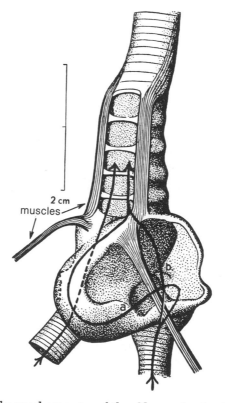

2 cm
muscles

Fig. 9.   The vocal apparatus of the oldsquaw has hardened into a
'drum'. The arrows indicate the direction of the air flowing from the
bronchi into the trachea. (After Rüppell, 1932, altered.)

The noises we have discussed so far are called instrumental noises. They stand in contrast to sounds produced in the syrinx, which lies at the lower end of the trachea. As we know, most vocal sounds of human beings and all other mammals are produced by the larynx, which lies at the upper end of the trachea. The avian syrinx lies inside the bird's body, right at the point where the trachea divides into two bronchi. In this region the cartilaginous rings of the bronchi, and often those of the trachea as well, are contracted, expanded, or modified in some other way. In many species the syrinx has been transformed into a bony drum with several fused rings. We find this kind of formation in ducks for example (Fig. 9). Species with such extraordinary modifications of their vocal apparatus have only fairly invariable vocalizations at their disposal. These birds must frequently assume 'compulsory stances' in order to be able to produce a specific sound. This is true of the turkey, for example, when he 'gobbles' and makes the sound *fum* (Fig. 10).

Sound arises in the syrinx at the tympaniform membranes (membranae tympaniformes). In the herring gull and many other species, these membranes are located in the vicinity of where the two main bronchi meet. The tympaniform membranes are stretched by muscles which are attached to the trachea. In the herring gull there are two pairs. The oscines have seven to nine pairs. The presence of many muscles in the sound apparatus betokens a rich vocal repertoire. But the Psittacidae, who are certainly well-endowed vocally, manage to get along with three pairs.

In order to comprehend the further prerequisites for sound production, we must pursue a bit of anatomy. Large portions of the avian body are interspersed with air sacs, which even extend into the hollow humerus and the sternum (Fig. 11). These air sacs are thin cutaneous structures which are dilatable, and which are in contact with the outside atmosphere above the lungs. One of their

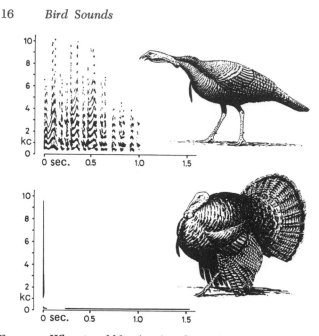

F<small>IG</small>. 10. When it gobbles (top) and goes *fum* (bottom), the turkey must assume the 'compulsory postures' depicted above. In
reality they are not stances but movements, caught by the drawer
at 0.5 second in each case. The *fum* sound is preceded by a brief
hiss, which shows up in the spectrogram as a vertical line at the left.
(After Schleidt, 1964.)

tasks is to ensure an efficient utilization of the air that is
breathed. One air sac surrounds the syrinx. With a simple
experiment Rüppell (1933) showed that the air sacs are
also very important in sound production. He stretched the
syrinx of a herring gull along with the trachea and the
bronchi in a glass chamber (Fig. 12). The air pressure
could be altered in the chamber by means of a tube.
When he sent a current of air through the bronchi, the
tympaniform membranes began to vibrate forcefully
along with the whole syrinx, the lower portion of the trachea, and the upper portion of the bronchi. But a vigorous
sound arose only when the air pressure in the glass chamber was increased at the same time. If there was no in-

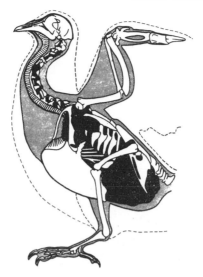

FIG. 11. Air sacs of the domestic pigeon (shaded). Lungs black. Flesh represented by dotted line. Bones white. (After B. Müller in Berndt/Meise, 1959.)

crease of air pressure in the chamber, the tympaniform membranes arched but did not produce any sound. This and other similar experiments indicate that the elasticity required for vibration is forced into the tympaniform membranes from the air sac which surrounds the syrinx.

A group of American researchers (Chamberlain et al., 1968) simplified the experiment in a basic way, using dead crows for the purpose. They opened one air sac and sucked air out from the trachea. That produced a partial vacuum in the syrinx, the tympaniform membranes arched inward, and the air current set them vibrating and ringing with sound.

In older geese the tympaniform membranes are stretched so tight that the air sac around the syrinx affects only timbre and pitch. Geese can call loudly even with a damaged air sac. Although the sound-producing membranes are stretched like the skins of a drum, they work

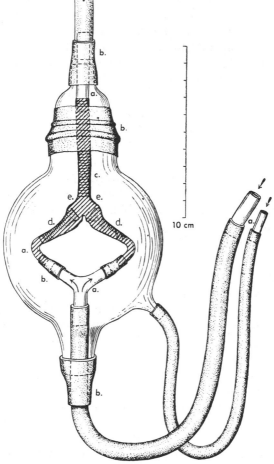

10 cm

Fig. 12. Vocal apparatus of the herring gull in a glass chamber:
(*a*) glass tubes, (*b*) rubber stoppers, (*c*) trachea, (*d*) bronchi, (*e*)
syrinx. (After Rüppell, 1933, altered.)

on the principle of a reed pipe. In other words, they peri-
odically obstruct or weaken a steady stream of air. The
reed pipes of an organ are built quite similarly. The pitch
of the sound produced in the syrinx depends on both the

pressure of the surrounding air sac and the force of the air current in the bronchi. This fact is easy enough to grasp. For the higher the pressure is in the air sac, the more the tympaniform membranes are stretched and the faster they vibrate. This gives rise to a higher tone, since we know that the pitch depends on the number of vibrations in a given period of time. But the strength of the air current in the syrinx also affects the vibratory amplitude of the tympaniform membrane as well as the range of vibration around it. Hence it also affects the loudness of the sound.

In most birds no noises arise in the larynx, which is at the upper end of the trachea. But in some birds hissing sounds do arise in the larynx. The clattering of the white stork, for example, may be introduced with such a hissing sound (Fig. 5).

But the structural features discussed above are not the only things responsible for the vocalizations produced by birds. As we noted earlier, the bird's sound apparatus operates on the principle of a reed pipe. Since musical instruments of this sort have an air tube and a connecting tube, e.g., a nozzle or mouthpiece, we should look for a similar setup in the avian body. More than a hundred years ago, Johannes Müller explored this point. He found the air tube in the bronchi and the connecting tube in the trachea and the oral region. After the air in the syrinx has started to vibrate through the tympaniform membrane and the surrounding area, the characteristic tone fades away faster when the damping is stronger. Aside from the spontaneous damping of the air itself, smooth surfaces have a weak damping effect whereas rough surfaces have a strong damping effect. A strong damping effect increases the range-area of the characteristic (intrinsic) tone, which consists primarily of a given pitch.

In the avian syrinx we should expect 'pure' tones to be a very rare occurrence (see page 2). Most of the time it is a mixture of different frequencies, which are also dampened differently in the connecting tube. The air in the trachea is forced to vibrate along by the sound source, i.e., the tympaniform membranes. We then talk about a 'coupling'. But in turn the air, which has been forced to join in the process of vibration, stimulates the tympaniform membranes, therefore, we get a 'back-coupling'. When this mutual influence and reinforcement is greater, the better the correspondence is between the range of the original tone in the tympaniform membrane and that in the trachea. Hence the length of the connecting tube—the trachea in this case—has a decisive influence on loudness, pitch, and timbre.

The length and shape of the avian trachea varies greatly, matching the variety of bird sounds. Sometimes the trachea is greatly elongated, as in the case of *Phonygammus keraudrenii* (one of the Paradisaeidae) which is the size of a mistle thrush. Although its larynx and syrinx are only 8–9 centimeters apart, the male's trachea is 50 centimeters long (Fig. 13). How this influences the very loud call of this bird is something we do not yet know in precise detail.

Like the connecting tube, the air tube of a reed instrument affects sound quality. This is also true in birds, whose air tube is the bronchi. The air sac around the syrinx serves as a resonance chamber. We do not know to what extent this holds true for the bird's whole body. Many species have developed special resonance chambers, in addition to the trachea and the expandable parts of the esophagus. The stork fashions a resonance chamber for its clatter by inflating its laryngeal membrane (Fig. 5). Before the sound exits from its beak, it is modified once again in the larynx and the back region of the mouth. Finally it is reinforced by the opened beak, which acts as a megaphone.

We have been considering the many ways in which a sound is influenced inside a bird before it is finally uttered. Essential factors are the pressure of the air sacs, the

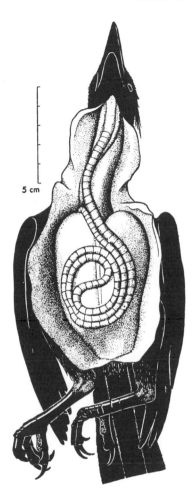

Fɪɢ. 13. The male trumpet bird has a greatly elongated trachea which influences its voice. (After Rüppell, 1933.)

elasticity of the tympaniform membrane, and the stretching of this membrane by muscles. Operating in close interaction are the vibrations of the tympaniform membrane, the trachea, and the bronchi. Finally, special resonance chambers, the size of the laryngeal passage, and the shape of the membrane also play a role. This brief commentary gives us an acquaintance with sound production inside a bird.

The ground-breaking explorations of Rüppell were far ahead of their time, for we did not learn anything new of an essential nature in the next 35 years. Only recently have a few researchers dared to tackle some hard, still unanswered questions. The views of one such researcher, an American named Stein, will be considered briefly in the next chapter.

III. *Open Questions about Sound Production*

Stein asked himself how a songbird manages to produce very rapid fluctuations in pitch which show up as zigzag lines on the spectrogram.

Among songbirds the carrier frequencies of such zigzag lines are quite high. Stein ascertained them at 3.2–8.4 kilocycles. The modulation frequency, on the other hand, lies between 90–300 c/s, i.e., 90–300 zags per second. There are various possible ways to produce such a high carrier frequency. One possibility would be to use the thinnest possible skin membrane. Since the internal tympaniform membrane is the thinnest part of the syrinx, in all likelihood it produces the carrier frequency. The pitch is modulated by the thicker and more solid external tympaniform membranes and the outer labia (Fig. 14). Since the left and right internal tympaniform membranes are not connected with each other, each of them could produce carrier frequencies. In other words they could 'sing' independently of each other offering a two-part vocal pattern or duet. With all the sounds investigated, pitch modulation and loudness modulation are correlated: the highest portions are also the loudest. This interplay is pre-

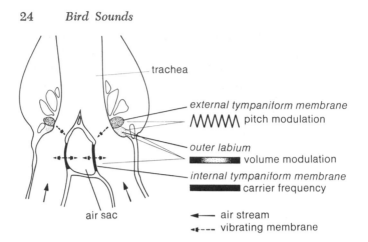

FIG. 14.   Longitudinal section through the syrinx of a songbird indicating the probable spots where the carrier frequency, pitch modulation, and volume modulation are produced. (After Stein, 1968, altered.)

sumably brought about from the same spot. Stein's considerations have not yet been proven, but they are supported by experiments with electronically produced tones.

Bird vocalizations are often very complicated. This is evident if we look at the strophe of a blackbird (Fig. 15). It begins its closing trill relatively low (a). In 1/100 of a second its call rises almost 3000 c/s, halts for half of 1/100 of a second, and then begins again almost 3000 c/s lower (b). This pattern is repeated twice more without interrup-

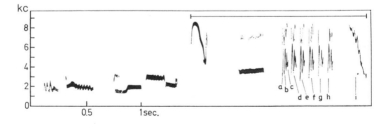

FIG. 15. Strophe of a blackbird. The last section (*a-i*) is very complicated.

tion, so that in the spectrogram we get a zigzag line whose pitch range narrows. The blackbird produces this 'trill' six times with only slight alterations, and these six trills do not even take a half-second. The final element attached to these trills begins at 8500 cycles per second. In 0.15 seconds it drops in a wavy line below 3000 cycles. This is no freak occurrence. The same male blackbird performs this artistic feat many times a day with unbelievable precision. And he maintains this strophe for years. Not satisfied with this, a male blackbird has at his disposal over 100 different strophes with more than 300 elements (Todt, 1968). When we compare this variety, precision, and complexity with what we know about sound production in the syrinx, the gaps in our knowledge are only too obvious.

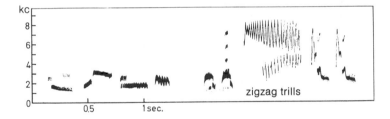

FIG. 16. Strophe of the same blackbird as in figure 15. The zigzag trill is a two-part vocal pattern.

Above we saw one possible explanation for the fact that birds can sing different things at the same time. Take the case of the male blackbird whose strophe is depicted in figure 15. The two zigzag trills in figure 16 move toward one another, hence the upper trill is not an 'overtone' of the lower one. If it were, it too would have to rise in pitch. Here we are in fact dealing with similar elements that are produced simultaneously. By the same token the compressed song of the great tit, which can be heard in early spring, tells us that this species can sing completely different things at the same time (Fig. 17). In fact this bird is capable of fashioning one sound out of four differ-

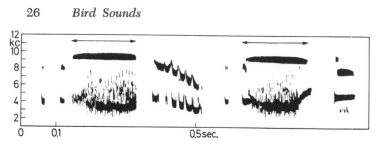

FIG. 17. Compressed song of the great tit (end of a strophe). At the points marked by a two-headed arrow the bird sings something completely different at the same time. The ratio between pitch scale and time scale in this illustration is different from any of the other illustrations.

ent tone bands running in four different directions. How he does that we do not know.

Another unsolved problem is the interplay of sound production and breathing. We do not know how a grasshopper warbler can sing up to 15 minutes without any large pauses at the mad pace of 54 elements per second. Needless to say, he must inhale and exhale as he sings. But how he keeps constant the air flow in his syrinx and the pressure in his air sacs is 'his secret'.

IV. *The Avian Ear and Its Contributions*

In general there is no ear opening to be seen on a bird's head. It is covered by feathers that are spread out and loosely arranged (Fig. 18). This format protects the sensitive components behind the feathers from air currents and foreign bodies during flight, without keeping out sounds to any great degree. Studies by Iljitschew and Iswekowa (1963) have shown that slippage of feathers over the ear openings seriously impairs acoustic permeability. In fact the molting of feathers around the ear has its own peculiarities. It lasts much longer than the molting of the other head feathers, so that there are always fully functional feathers in front of the ear.

Many birds can raise the feathers on the back edge of their ear to some extent. This serves to funnel sound into the ear even better, and it is abetted by the close-knit construction of the feathers there (Fig. 18). The Strigidae have movable skin folds on the back edge of the ear, and frequently on the front edge of the ear as well. They can move these folds at will, thereby closing the ear opening or placing it perpendicular to the sound source. The skin folds then collect the sound in a funnel, just as a cat's ears or our own do. The ear openings of some owl species ac-

FIG. 18.   From left to right, feather of the bullfinch from the back edge of the ear (sound-funnelling), from its crown (normal feather), and from in front of the ear (sound-transmitting). Approximately 5 times magnification. (After Schwartzkopff, 1955.)

tive at night are asymmetrical (Fig. 19). Indeed so are the connected bones of Tengmalm's owl. This probably improves their ability to zero in on a sound source.

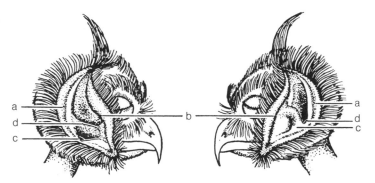

FIG. 19.   Asymmetry of the external ear opening of the long-eared owl: (*a*) back ear flap, (*b*) front ear flap, (*c*) ear entrance, (*d*) bridge (fold of connective tissue). (After Schwartzkopff, 1965.)

At the end of the auditory canal lies the tympanum, to which the ear bone or columella is fused (Fig. 20). In birds it is one piece whereas in human beings there are three such bones: malleus, incus, and stapes. Elastic extensions and a tendon give the columella the guidance it needs for its piston-like motions. The basal plate of the

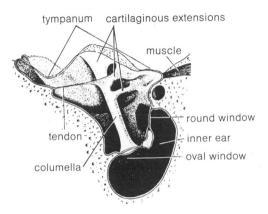

FIG. 20.   Ear of the domestic fowl. (After Pohlmann in Berndt/ Meise, 1959, altered.)

columella seals off the oval window to the inner ear. The inner ear, known as the cochlea, is filled with lymph. The term 'cochlea', which means 'snail', derives from the way this part of the ear is constructed in human beings. In reality the avian cochlea is not snail-like but only slightly curved. Within the cochlea lie the auditory sense organs. A sound impression arises through the vibration of air particles. It is taken in by the tympanum and transmitted across the columella, through the oval window, into the fluid of the inner ear. In this process the round window provides for pressure balance. Since the tympanum takes up a greater area than the oval window, the impression taken in is intensified. This is necessary for several reasons, one being to balance off the stronger damping effect of the liquid-filled inner ear as opposed to that of the air.

Pressure intensification is one index of auditory capacity and performance.

Neither the dimensions nor the mass of the columella are left to chance by nature. They are precisely right for undistorted sound transmission. It is all the more astonishing that the avian ear, whose performance is equal to our own and better in some ways, is built more simply. That is true not only of the sound-conducting apparatus but also of the inner ear. We know relatively little about the way stimuli are received and relayed in the sensory cells of the avian cochlea, as compared with these same processes in our own ear.

The hearing range of birds, and hence their vocal sounds, correspond pretty much to ours. That is the reason why bird sounds have been a favorite subject of research for such a long time. If the signals emitted by some species of animal lie completely outside our perceptual capabilities, e.g., many bat sounds and insect perfumes, or even if it is simply a matter of them being emitted in another medium, e.g., fish sounds, our very knowledge of their existence is very slow in coming. For example, we could entertain the wholly erroneous notion that fish are mute.

The lowest sound that a bird can perceive is around 40 cycles per second. For human beings it is around 16 cycles per second. The upper limits for most birds, and for us too, is 10,000 to 20,000 c/s. But a few species hear 30,000 c/s if the sound is loud enough.

The hearing of the bullfinch ranges from below 100 c/s to 25,000 c/s. Its ear is most readily attuned to those pitches which convey particularly important biological information. On the basis of figure 21 this would seem to come down to its song and a few calls. Although the points on the auditory graph are spaced quite far apart, they agree quite well with the findings of sound-spectrogram analysis.

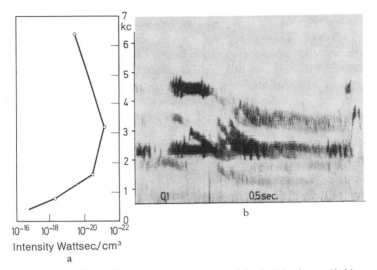

FIG. 21 *a* and *b*. The greatest receptivity of the bullfinch ear (left) lies at 300 c/s. That is also the intermediate pitch range of its own voice (right). (*a*, after Schwartzkopff, 1960, altered. *b*, ten song spectrograms overlaid.)

Dovetailing with the noises emitted by their prey, the greatest sensitivity of many owl species lies around 6000 c/s. Whereas the receptivity of the avian ear corresponds with that of the human ear to a large extent, the night-hunting species of owl surpass us in that respect. Their ability to determine direction and distance also displays greater precision than ours. Tengmalm's owl, for example, is capable of locating a mouse acoustically at a distance of 70 meters (Kuhk, 1966).

Very few people know the barn owl which flies over their house every night. It is on its way from its fledglings in the church loft to hunt for mice, rats, and shrews in the nearby meadows and fields. But after only a few summer nights, an expert knows whether there is a barn owl in the neighborhood. Its distinctive snoring gives it away.

One would think that mice would be safe from the barn owl on moonless nights. But this is not so. The barn owl can lay hold of its prey in total darkness. The rustle of the mouse's scurrying is enough to lead the barn owl to it. Payne (1962) proved this in a number of experiments. He pulled a paper mouse across the leaf-covered floor of a room in complete darkness; the paper mouse was snatched up by the barn owl with the same sureness that a live mouse is grabbed. He played the sound of rustling leaves over a loudspeaker; the loudspeaker became the prey. He tied a dry leaf to a mouse's tail and let it run over a sandy surface; the owl grabbed the leaf. There is a parallax involved here: the owl hears the mouse with his ear but must grab it with his talons. Yet he makes the compensation effortlessly. Right from the start of his flight, his head is pointed in the direction of the noise. Only at the last moment before reaching his prey does he pull his feet up in front of him so that they are aligned

FIG. 22. The outer edges of the tawny owl's wing feathers are fringed. This contributes to noiseless flight. (After Rutschke, 1966.)

with the direction-line maintained by his head. At least two sounds or noises must come from his prey before the barn owl starts his flight. From these bits of information the bird 'calculates' the direction and the distance involved. In doing this he pinpoints not only the terminus of the noise but also the direction in which the mouse is moving; for the claw imprints always lie at a right angle to the longitudinal axis of the mouse. If one ear of the barn owl is plugged up, it will still fly in the right direction, but it will miss the mouse because it can no longer judge the distance correctly.

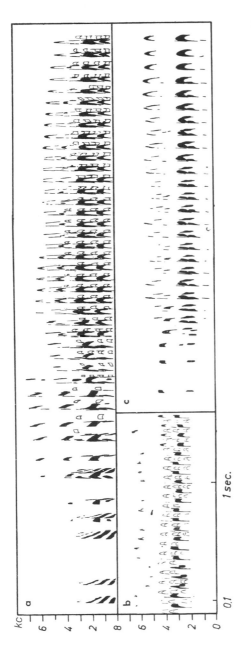

Fig. 23 a-c. Song of the little grebe: (a) and (b) both partners of a pair, (c) one bird alone. In (a) one bird (black) begins erratically; after the eighth element the second bird (white) steps in. The second bird begins precisely when the first bird stops even though the first bird sings slowly at first, picks up speed as he goes along, and then slows down again toward the end. (b) portion of a longer trill duet. (After Bandorf, 1968, and Thielcke.)

Someone observing a dense swarm of starlings flying by will certainly be impressed by their wing noises. In chapter 2 we pointed out that feather noises can be signals for a species group. The next step in making such signals even more impressive is the transformation of certain feathers into sound-producing ones, as we saw in the case of the snipe (page 11). The owls have taken the opposite course: they fly noiselessly. This is important in two respects. Firstly, their own hearing is not impaired by flight noises. Secondly, their prey cannot perceive them. Owls fly soundlessly because their outer wing feathers are notched at the outer edge (Fig. 22), frayed on the inner side, and padded with down on top. In short, their feathers are constructed quite the opposite to solid sound-producing feathers. By contrast, the African fishing owl lacks these structures. Since it feeds on fishes and crabs, it can 'afford' to make noise in flight.

While birds can distinguish pitches just about as well as we can, their acoustic time resolution is much better than ours. The little grebe has a song in which both partners frequently take part. The second participant joins in and dovetails its song completely with that of the first singer, making the appropriate changes in speed with hair-splitting precision (Fig. 23). The interval between their segments amounts to a thirtieth of a second. Comparisons of original song and its imitations compel us to assume that birds can resolve and analyze far more acoustic impressions in a given span of time than we can.

V. By Their Songs You Shall Know Them

If you were to head outdoors with a bird expert, you would probably be surprised to hear him say something like this: "Over there a marsh tit is singing, that drumming sound is coming from a great spotted woodpecker, and a blackbird is making that 'chak' sound." The trained ornithologist can say all this without even seeing the bird in question.

This is possible only because the vocal sounds of birds and animals in general are peculiar to a given species. If a person devotes long enough time to a given animal group, he will be able to distinguish species on the basis of their sounds just as well as on the basis of their appearance. Indeed sound patterns are often better suited to provide identification than are bodily features. We shall examine more of them later.

Right now let us return to our singing marsh tit. We notice that it is no longer 'chattering' (Fig. 24 a–c). The same male suddenly sings a completely different strophe. If we are patient long enough, we may notice him shifting to a third kind of strophe. The three types of strophes are very different (Fig. 24). If one did not know they came

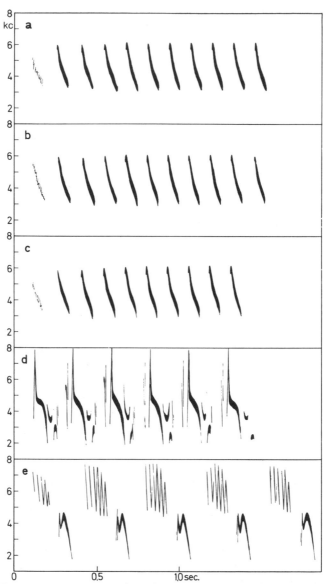

FIG. 24 *a–e*. Five strophes of one and the same male marsh tit: (*a–c*) three strophes of the first type, (*d*) one strophe of a second type, (*e*) one strophe of a third type.

from the same bird, one might well take them to be the songs of different species.

The same male marsh tit sings strophes of the same type in a very uniform way (Fig. 24 a–c). The song differences between different males are greater (Fig. 25), but in principle it is always a slight variation on the same pattern. For this reason we will always recognize the song of the marsh tit as that of the marsh tit, once we have gotten the different strophe types into our head. The same holds true for the other species.

As different as the three song types of the marsh tit are, they also have something in common. Within a strophe there is a stereotyped repetition of either one element, e.g., the chatter strophe of figure 24 a–c, or of a group of elements, e.g., the strophe of figure 24 d, e. With greater or lesser deviations, almost all the investigated songs of genuine tits are fashioned in the same way (cf. Fig. 77). Only one species, a South Asian relative of the European coal tit, diverges from this pattern in a fundamental way. Furthermore, it is characteristic of all tits without exception that they sing one strophe type for awhile and then proceed to another—insofar as they have more than one. Despite these shared characteristics, the species-specific quality is guaranteed by continually novel element patterns and their associated timbres.

Other avian species have a different strophe structure. Most short-toed treecreepers sing six different elements in the same sequence. The male has at most two types of strophes. In figure 26 we have a comparison between five different males from two different regions (Ludwigsburg in southern Germany and La Granja in central Spain). Within a given region the songs of males are very uniform. And even from one region to another we find that the differences are generally slight. The males in La Granja differ most from the other 450 males recorded.

Different again is the strophe structure of the chiffchaff. His monotonous song is very striking and easily remem-

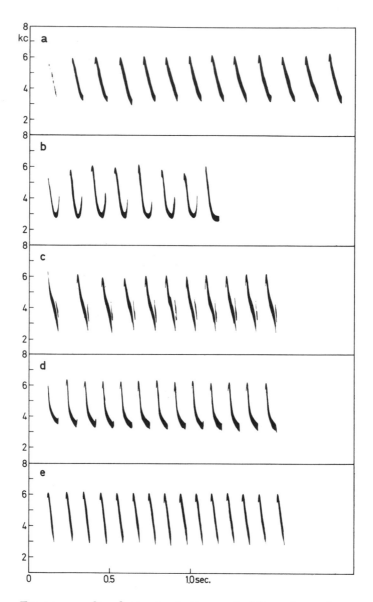

FIG. 25 *a–e*.   One chatter strophe from each of five male marsh tits.

bered. To be sure, it consists of nothing more than 'chiff chaff', which accounts for its name. But a male can have up to nine different elements, which are arranged in the individual strophes in varying sequence (Fig. 27). In our example there are four elements. The strophes are of very different length. A characteristic peculiar to the chiffchaff is the fact that the interval from one element to the next is very constant. This feature is lacking in other species which have a corresponding strophe structure.

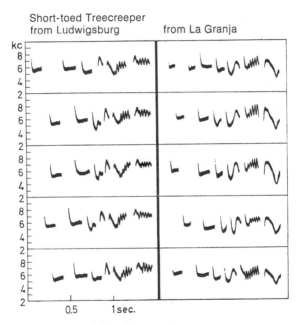

Fig. 26. Strophes of five short-toed treecreepers in southern Germany (left) and five short-toed treecreepers in central Spain (right). Within a given population the song is very stereotyped.

We studied some samples of blackbird song on page 24. A male can have over a hundred different strophes. But blackbird song differs from that of the marsh tit and that of the short-toed treecreeper not only in its number and variety but also in the variegated succession of its stro-

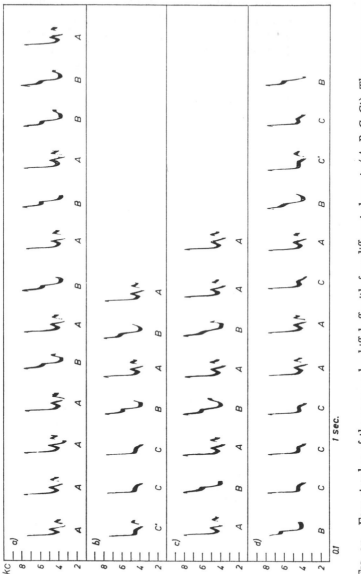

Fig. 27. Four strophes of the same male chiffchaff with four different elements (A, B, C, C'). The song can vary greatly in the length of its strophes and the succession of elements.

phes. Parts of a blackbird strophe can crop up in another strophe—as is always the case in chiffchaff strophes.

By discussing the songs of the marsh tit, the short-toed treecreeper, the chiffchaff, and the blackbird, I have provided one example of each of the four different principles on which songs are constructed. Almost all bird songs are composed in this way.

VI. *The Functions of Bird Song*

If we tape the song of a male chiffchaff and play it back to the same bird, or to another male chiffchaff, we will witness an astonishing reaction. As if drawn by a magnet, the chiffchaff flies in the direction of the loudspeaker, hovers briefly near it with wings fluttering furiously, and then gives his answer to the song coming through the loudspeaker. First he utters a very hastily delivered strophe that almost sounds like a stammer. Then gradually he shifts into his normal song, which he reiterates a bit more frequently than he did before the experiment began. Once I observed an aroused chiffchaff hacking away at the diaphragm of my loudspeaker. The explanation was clear to be seen: the chiffchaff thought he was dealing with an intruder who had invaded his preserve.

In the spring male birds take possession of some patch of woodland, some lane, hedge, or meadow. When they do, they make every effort to keep out other males of the same species by a great deal of singing. Wandering males thus know right away where they can find a suitable patch of living space that is free of rivals. At the start of the breeding period there is much conflict between males of the same species. But once the boundaries of a bird's territory have been set up, its song alone usually suffices to protect and preserve its property. Some say that bird song saves energy because it forestalls debilitating conflicts, but we do not really know whether this is correct. What is certain is that a singing bird is much easier to notice in an ill-defined countryside than is a mute bird.

The song of a male bird speaks not only to males but also to females of the same species. In our region male birds take possession of their precinct in the spring and then use their song to attract the attention of eligible females at a distance. In general, unmated males sing more than mated ones. We do not know whether female birds can make out the status of males from this. Nor indeed do we know much for sure about the way in which song works to attract females. Once the pair has found each other, the male sings much less than before. And he seems to prefer to sing when his mate is out of his sight. Thus bird song serves to keep the pair together.

The pekin robin of China, also known as the china nightingale, has two different song-forms (Fig. 28). One is briefer and less variable; with this the male maintains contact with his partner. The other song-form is used primarily for territorial display. If we separate the members of a pair, the male will start up his contact strophe and the female will begin a special call series. In this way they make vocal contact and quickly get together again. In these sounds they probably recognize each other as individuals. Since they mate permanently, such personal recognition is necessary. The unchanging nature of the strophe over the course of many years (Fig. 28 f–k) must contribute greatly to this end.

Barbara Brockway (1962) discovered another social function of bird song among the budgerigars. Eggs were laid by females who simply heard males of their own species but could not see them. Eggs were not laid by females who had no auditory contact with males. From these studies one may conclude that species-specific vocalizations bring males and females together in reproductive behavior. In further investigations Barbara Brockway discovered which sounds are decisive for this purpose. It is the soft song before copulation—sung six times each day—that induces the female to lay eggs.

The experiment with chiffchaff strophes, described at the beginning of this chapter, pointed up its ability to stimulate the male's attention and intensify his rate of song. This stimulation has been confirmed by many experiments. Since this leads to regular song duels between neighbors of the same species, this mutual stimulation to pick up the beat may well help to coordinate the course of the breeding period for a whole group. Lott and others (1967) have demonstrated this in connection with the sounds arising in the colony milieu of the ring dove.

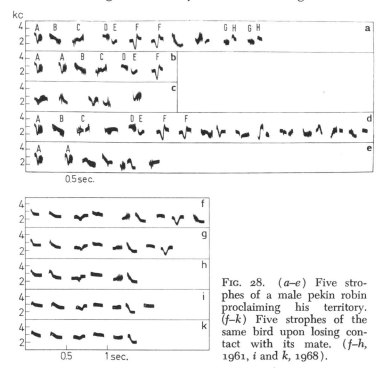

Fig. 28. (*a–e*) Five strophes of a male pekin robin proclaiming his territory. (*f–k*) Five strophes of the same bird upon losing contact with its mate. (*f–h*, 1961, *i* and *k*, 1968).

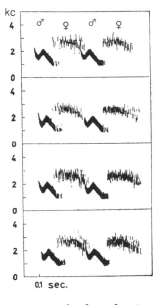

FIG. 29. Alternating song of male and female pair of black-headed gonoleks. (After a recording made by G. Niethammer.)

In our region, as far as we know, it is the lengthening period of daylight that induces all individuals of a species to succumb to a reproductive mood at approximately the same time. In tropical regions, however, other factors would seem to be at work. There, birds often do not breed in the spring. Some may breed at the beginning of the rainy season, for example, while others do so toward the end of the rainy season. It may well be that the pair are attuned to each other by the antiphonal songs and duets which are frequent in the tropics. What is more, these forms of song may well be necessary for maintaining the unity of the pair in the dense areas of tropical jungle and reeds, as well as being necessary for nocturnal species. We have already examined a duet of astonishing precision in an earlier chapter (Fig. 23).

Thus song exercises very important functions in the reproductive behavior of the bird. It points out territory, probably leads females to eligible males, holds the pair together, and attunes partners or a whole group to one another. At least one of these functions should be fulfilled if we are talking about song.[1] Bird song generally consists of strophes (cf. Fig. 24) which are composed of several or many elements. The term 'song' should be applied to single elements with one of the aforementioned functions only if a species lacks vocalizations which can be divided into strophes.

The grassfinches, favorite cage birds in Europe, differ from most other avian species insofar as they never broadcast territorial possession with their song. Instead they sing at mating time, and the Africans among them maintain contact with their mates thereby (Harrison, 1962). Like the pekin robin, the male Purple Grenadier has two song forms at its disposal, one being used for mating and the other for vocal contact (Nicolai, 1962). The summoning function is absent in the songs of Australian grassfinches. To maintain the colony, the Asiatic spicefinch and the Australian species of the same genus sing in chorus—several males sitting in feather contact (Moynihan and Hall, 1954; also Immelmann, 1962). Indeed some species from Africa and Australia have an 'audience'. When a male sings his song, males and females of the species stretch their ears and extend their necks toward him. Immelmann (1962) sees this behavior as a means of solidifying the maintenance of the colony.

In most cases a specific strophe of a male bird, or his whole repertoire, is characteristic of him alone. Even the male of species with a very stereotyped strophe and pronounced dialects can be distinguished from all the males in his neighborhood by fine details. Judith Weeden and Falls (1959) have shown that this disparity can be significant in a bird's life. The American ovenbird uses it to

---

1. By contrast song that is not fully developed—among juveniles, and among adults outside the mating season—usually lacks these functions completely. Here we call them respectively 'juvenile song' and 'winter song'.

distinguish between his neighbors and foreigners. They react much more fiercely to foreigners because the latter are in search of a territory while their neighbors already possess one. Residents have no reason to put up a serious fight for another preserve. Once the territorial boundary lines are fixed, the daily song duels near these boundaries serve more as confirmation than as a proclamation of hostile intentions. As is so often the case with different members of the same species living together, it becomes a matter of ritual.

VII. *How a Bird Recognizes Its Song*

In chapter 1 we saw how the strophe of a yellowhammer looked on a sound spectrogram (Fig. 2). Yellowhammers sing one strophe in a fairly stereotyped fashion and then shift to another strophe type. A male yellowhammer can have up to four different types of strophes. The strophes of one particular type are as uniform as those of the marsh tit.

Of the strophe types which I recorded from 28 males, no two are similar enough to be associated with one type; but all the strophes are built on the same principle (Fig. 30). The major part of the strophe is composed of homogeneous elements which follow one another at precise intervals and are almost always bipartite. The first is soft, the succeeding ones become louder and louder. Often the strophe ends with one or two long drawn out elements. These may be absent altogether, but they are never sung alone.

The simple structure of the yellowhammer's strophe and the good reaction of the male to a song recorded on tape and played back to him offer us a challenge. Can we investigate the significance of the individual components of his song by further experiments?

I myself have played ten recordings of a yellowhammer strophe, each artificially altered in a different way, to yellowhammers living in the wild. I also played the song of the cirl bunting, a close relative of the yellowhammer. In every case it is only male yellowhammers that have reacted. The altered strophe was played to each male ten times. Then, after a pause, the unaltered strophe was played to each male ten times. In this case the unaltered strophe was one without the closing element mentioned above, which is absent from many strophes anyhow. The columns in figure 31 indicate how many males were attracted by the altered strophe, if one equates the impact of the unaltered strophe with 100. The second experiment (B) indicates the usefulness of the method, for two sets of unaltered strophes were given practically the same response. The yellowhammer does not react completely just to the first set, or only to the second set.

Protracting the strophe by doubling the number of bipartite elements (Fig. 31 A) does not impair its effectiveness any more than replacing a steadily increasing volume with a fluctuating volume (31 C). Filtering out undertones below 4000 c/s and overtones above 6500 c/s is also of secondary importance (31 D). Thus the part of these overtones in timbre is slight in the song of the yellowhammer. This fits in with our acoustic impression of the altered strophe. The overtones of our musical instruments, by contrast, contribute greatly to the timbre.

The first astonishing thing we note is that the strophe is so effective when played backwards (31 E). Instead of increasing steadily, the volume drops; and the fine details of the individual elements come in reverse order. But this is explicable because in different strophes the double elements can begin with the lower part (Fig. 30 a) or with the higher part (Fig. 30 c), and intensity is insignificant

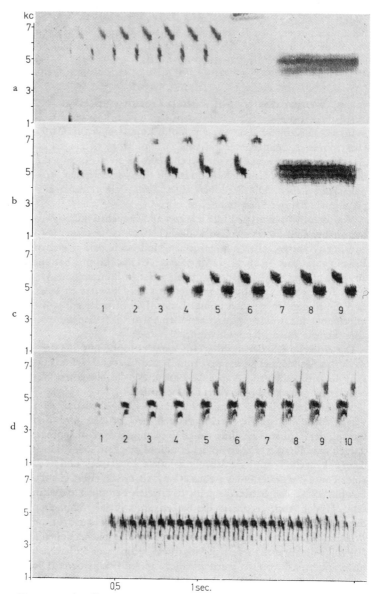

FIG. 30. (a–d) One strope of each of four male yellowhammers.
(e) The strophe of a male cirl bunting. Strophes (c–e) were played
to yellowhammers in the wild.

Strophe in Fig. 30		n	Type of Alteration	0 20 40 60 80 100 120
A	c	7	18 double elements instead of 9	
B	d	19	Unaltered	
C	c	7	No continuing increase in loudness	
D	c	10	Overtones and under-tones filtered out	
E	d	20	Strophe backwards	
F		24	Long drawn out element by itself, as in figure 30b	
G	c	16	Pitch raised 2 kc	
H	c	8	Pitch lowered 1 kc	
I	d	20	Last double element alone	
K	d	19	Elements 2, 3, 5, 6, 8, 9 erased	
L	c	18	Pitch lowered 2 kc	
M	e	20	Strophe of another species	

FIG. 31. Results of experiment with dummy strophes on yellow-hammers in the wild. First ten strophes altered in the same way were played to a given male, then ten unaltered strophes. The number of males attracted by the unaltered strophe is equated with 100 (dash line). The number of males attracted by the altered strophe is in proportion to that (columns). In (*B*) two unaltered strophes were played to the same male, each one ten times. The almost identical reaction to both series indicates the usefulness of the method.

on the basis of test A in figure 31. Chiffchaffs generally do not react to their song when it is played backwards to them. In this case the character of the individual elements is indeed altered in a fundamental way.

About sixty percent of the yellowhammers indicate by their behavior that they recognize the closing element as characteristic of them alone (31 F). Almost the same number of males accept pitch alterations of plus 2 kilocycles (31 G) or minus 1 kilocycle (31 H). But when the pitch drops 2 kilocycles (31 L), the strophe has no more effect on them than that of another species (31 M). The dummied sound strophes, which were altered in pitch, were not distorted in terms of time.

Another surprise is that one double element by itself (31 I), and also four with big pauses (31 K), were generally recognized as characteristic of the species.

In the previous chapter we noted that females as well as males are attracted by the song of the species. It is quite conceivable that the former measure the song by different standards. As studies by Weeden and Falls (1959) have indicated, the American ovenbird can distinguish neighbors from foreigners. If yellowhammers were in a position to do this, they could use other characteristic features of their song for this purpose. Here again we know very little, as is so often the case with bird sounds. Apart from the species cited above, only a few studies are available. The most detailed one is Bremond's study (1968) of the robin.

VIII. *Calls*

So far we have been concentrating on bird songs. We have seen how they are constructed, what possibilities for variation are available to the individual bird, what members of the same species can gather from them, and how they recognize the song of their species.

This, however, does not exhaust a bird's repertoire. For besides song they also have calls (sometimes called 'cries') at their disposal. For the most part these calls perform different social functions than song. Calls are usually short, and on the spectrogram they look like a single element of a bird's song. Now for this reason one might think that avian calls can be easily distinguished from avian song, but that is not always the case. A single element, whose form cannot be distinguished from that of a call, can be a bird's complete song. On the other side of the coin, a call can be combined and integrated with other calls so that they sound like 'primitive' song strophes. So we have no alternative but to investigate the social import of a given vocal sound in order to classify it as a call or a song; and even then we encounter borderline cases. We have already seen what purposes are served by song in the social life of the bird (chapter 6). The repertoire of calls

53

varies greatly from species to species. A white stork has three calls at its disposal, a song bird can have up to twenty. Our domestic fowl, in fact, has twenty-six calls.

a) Signals from egg to egg

Avian species whose clutch size consists of many eggs generally lay one egg per day. But they begin to brood before all the eggs have been laid. And even though the eggs laid last are incubated for a shorter time, the young of many species hatch within a few hours. How that is possible has been a much debated question. Only in recent years have people hit upon the idea that the young chicks themselves might be capable of bringing about this astonishing synchronization. This idea has been proposed by Goethe (1955) and Margaret Vince (1964, 1966, 1967, 1968).

The young of the bobwhite quail normally hatch on the twenty-third day of incubation. From the twentieth day on they make a peeping sound. After that they begin to make a clicking sound. These rhythmic noises arise in the process of breathing, and they are dropped a few hours after hatching. The time interval between the first peep and the first click varies greatly with each individual chick, ranging from one hour to forty-three hours. By contrast, the range of variation from the first click to hatching time is very small, amounting to no more than about six hours. Finally, at hatching time there are also typical noises.

Chicks still in the egg, placed in an incubator one day later than other eggs in the clutch, began to peep twenty-four hours later. But they began their clicking sound only a few hours after the others did—a few hours at most. And all of them were hatched within a short span of time, as is the case when the eggs are incubated by the mother. When Vince placed the eggs ten centimeters apart in the incubator, they hatched in a period of forty-six hours. Eggs lying in contact required only six hours.

If we compare the findings on the three vocal sounds—peep, click, hatching sounds—it is the click that appears to be the most likely synchronizer in the hatching process.

Vince now went a step further in her investigation. She took eggs of the bobwhite quail and of *Coturnix coturnix* and exposed them to vibrations or recorded click sounds which would be appropriate under natural hatching conditions. Both methods led to premature hatching. The clicking sound accelerates the hatching of far developed bobwhites. Here it appears to be merely a byproduct of breathing. Young tree sparrows and great tits make clicking sounds just as ducks and quails do, but they do not synchronize their hatching. Only a few species have turned this call, which originally had no social function, into a socially useful thing.

The eggs and fledglings of many ground-breeding species are delicacies in the eyes of predators. When the female is incubating quietly on her nest, the danger is relatively small. But once the first young have hatched, they offer many clues to the sharp eyes of crow and kite, who may decide to investigate the nest area more closely. The hatching time from first fledgling to last is especially critical because the mother must both incubate eggs and care for her young fledglings. Any shortening of this period would scarcely be regarded as a loss. That is probably the reason why some birds have come to make social use of their click sounds—in addition to natural selection.

b) *Common murres learn inside the egg*

The visitor to Helgoland at breeding time will run into a black and white bird about the size of a mallard, who has a long, pointed beak. There on the steep rocks it will be breeding in a colony of about 1000 pairs. The first German-speaking visitors apparently had no high opinion of this bird. They considered it rather dumb—hence the German names 'Dumme Lumme' and 'Trottellumme'. Once upon a time there were about 4000 pairs on Helgoland,

and to this day you can find a colony of about 100,000 pairs on a Fjord in Arctic Norway.

Common murres (*Uria aalge*) prefer to lay their eggs on a shelf of the steep, craggy rocks where they will be safe from land predators. Space on the steep cliffs is scanty, hence there is not much distance between the brooding birds (Fig. 32). Brooding in colonies offers advantages to many species, but it also has its disadvantages. For example, there is the problem of finding one's own young again after some disturbance. If common murres were to take in the first egg they chanced upon, a high survival rate of young generation would not be possible. The common murres have found a surprising solution for this problem, and Tschanz (1968) discovered their secret in a number of experiments. He set up his research post on the Island of Vedøy, one of the Lofoten Islands. It is a group of islands off the Norwegian coast that lies north of the Arctic Circle.

When there is some disturbance around the nest, the adult birds fly away and the young hide in the rocky crevices. When the adults return, they find the rocky shelf empty. They then emit a series of calls, which is different for each common murre. The difference can be seen clearly on the sound spectrogram (Fig. 33). The young respond and run, by preference, to their parents. In a short time each fledgling is back under its own 'radiator'.

To know which adults and fledglings belong together, one must mark them individually. Tschanz and his co-workers did this. Only then could they state that parents and fledglings get back together after some disturbance.

Normally the adult common murres fly away when a human being drops down on their rocky shelf. But one female did not do this, remaining with her chick instead. With her help Tschanz performed an instructive experiment. He recorded her summons call to the chick on tape and played it back to mother and chick. With that the chick came out from under its parent's wing and headed

Fig. 32.   Common murres brood as close to each other as they are standing here. (Photo by B. Tschanz.)

for the loudspeaker. When mother called and the tape was turned off, the chick headed back to its mother. But when its mother's call sounded on the tape again, the chick headed once more for the apparatus. The chick sauntered back and forth several times in this fashion. Finally it tried to slip under the recorder, because the latter was calling more than its flesh-and-blood relative. Many such experiments were tried out with fledglings on the cliff. They were presented with recordings of their

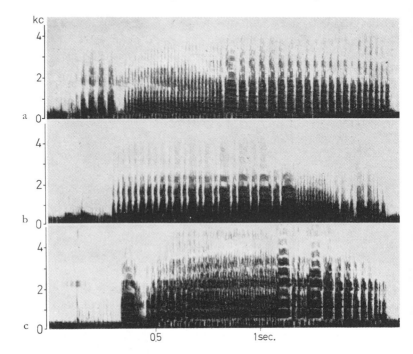

FIG. 33.   In the sound-contact calls of the adult birds the young common murres recognize their parents personally. (*a–c*) Sound-contact calls of three adult birds. (From tape recordings by B. Tschanz.)

own parents' calls and of calls by other common murres. The result was the same. Common murre chicks recognize the personal feeding call of their own parents right after they have hatched. There was real grounds for the surmise that they had come to know it while they were still in the egg. But before we describe some experiments dealing with this matter, let us note Tschanz's observations on the behavior of parents and chicks in the last days before the eggs are actually hatched.

Between 2 1/2 and 4 1/2 days before hatching, one can hear a scraping sound and a soft peep coming from inside the egg. A few hours after the first peep, a tiny triangular hole or a network of fine cross hatching appears near the blunt end of the egg. The chick presses itself against the egg wall and thereby breaks off a few more pieces of the egg shell lying on top of its beak. The little peck hole is enlarged into a breathing hole. Now, millimeter by millimeter, the young chick turns on its longitudinal axis and 'saws' with its eye tooth, i.e., a small, calcareous protuberance on the tip of its beak. A groove appears, and before the chick has turned full circle it slips out of the shell cover it has been fashioning. Hatching is complete. For this operation the chick needs 3 days and 14 hours. During this period it is not at work continuously, operating instead in spurts. While it is working to break open the shell, the chick calls out a great deal. It has no less than three calls, which profoundly affect the behavior of its parents. This provokes calls from them in turn, and these latter calls are of great importance to the fledglings.

From the first to the twenty-eighth day of brooding, the common murres are quiet and still while they brood. Every 16 to 24 hours, the partners alternate. When the first sounds come from inside the egg, the behavior of the parents changes. They stand up 'nervously', peer at the egg, emit their feeding call, bring fish and try to feed the egg, and alternate shifts more frequently. Some behavior patterns—preening, wing flapping, picking up and dropping nest material—suggest conflict situations to the observer. The shift and adaptation of the parents from the egg to the fledgling calls for many new reactions. Some small mistake could be fatal to the youngster. It is important for the parents to adapt to the new situation as early as possible.

Here voice contact between parents and chick plays an important role. In the period when the parents are making preparations for the hatching, they call to the chicks more often. More important, they prefer to emit their call when the chick is 'at work' inside the egg or emitting a call of its own. And the chicks respond more frequently to their parents' call during the phase when they are fashioning a peck hole and enlarging it into a breathing hole. Tschanz took common murres in an incubator and, once they had uttered their first peep, played five similar calls to them every hour. The result was astonishing. During the phase when they were working on the breathing hole inside the egg, they could already clearly distinguish the training call from other calls, and they also learned to distinguish a second call. Thus common murres know their parents even before they have seen them, and this 'personal relationship' arises in a purely acoustical way. It becomes significant only after the chicks have hatched—when it is a matter of feeding the chicks or bringing parents and chicks back together after some disturbance.

Under natural conditions the chicks learn to recognize their parents personally only through their feeding calls, even though the parents emit other calls as well. Even the feeding calls of neighboring common murres have no effect, even though their calls may sound just as loud to the chick in the egg as its parents' call does. Apparently the learning readiness of the chick is very great during the phases when it is at work itself, for it is then that it listens to the feeding call of its own parents by preference.

If one plays the training call and some other feeding call to a newly hatched chick at the same time, it will usually head for the speaker that is emitting the training call. But if one plays only some unfamiliar feeding call, the chick will react to that too. This facilitates the adoption of orphaned chicks that are not one's own. All that it takes is five feedings associated with a new call, and the fledglings will respond to the new call as they did to the old one—without losing their attachment to the latter.

The behavior of the common murre has only a few basic similarities with personal relationships as we know them among human beings. It has a solid learning capability which enables the fledgling common murre, while still in the egg and otherwise quite helpless, to form an attachment to its parents. The common murre is not so dumb after all.

c) *The turkey hen kills her silent chicks*

For turkey chicks, their first cheep is a matter of life and death. If they remain silent, they are treated as nest enemies. Turkey chicks are never mute, of course, so this never happens. But W. Schleidt, Margret Schleidt, and Monica Magg (1960) set up an artificial situation by deafening some turkey hens. During the period of mating and brooding, these hens acted quite normal. But as soon as their chicks had hatched, and they felt them moving around underneath them, they pecked their fledglings to death. Chicks outside the reach of mother's beak provoked her to defensive behavior patterns designed to ward off nest enemies. The hen's back feathers bristled, and she spread her tail. But when an egg was placed in the same spot, she rolled it into the nest.

These results are all the more astonishing in the light of the fact that the turkey's eyes are not underdeveloped by any means. On the contrary they, like almost all birds, can see very well. Anyone can verify this fact by watching turkeys hunt for grasshoppers.

In many areas of avian life, optical and acoustical signals work together. In many cases it is only the combined impact of both sensory realms that triggers a complete, full-blown reaction. Apparently turkeys can only distinguish between small nest robbers and their own offspring on the basis of what they hear. Cheeping initiates brood-

ing behavior, chicks that remain silent provoke hostile behavior. This does not mean that the cheeping has to come
from turkey chicks by any means, for normal turkey hens
are favorite foster mothers for many sorts of fowl. They
will take charge of chicklings and ducklings as readily as
they will take charge of the young of their own species—
despite the somewhat different sounds emitted by the
other species. This forces us to conclude that the triggers
for their nursing behavior are extraordinarily unspecified
and featureless. But this development may have taken
place in the process of domestication.

d) A mother duck leads her small fry

Duckling sounds in the egg may well contribute to another process, helping the parents to prepare for their new
task of caring for their young. Many precocial birds are
faced with the problem of keeping a crowd of small fry
together and leading them to good feeding grounds that
are safe from their enemies. The young ducklings have at
least two calls with which to make their feelings known.
When everything is going fine, they continually emit a
sound-contact call. It is their way of saying: "I'm here,
everything is going great." But if they lose sight of their
brothers and sisters, they emit a shrill cry to indicate their
abandonment. Lorenz (1935) vividly describes the reactions of a mother mallard to this cry:

Upon hearing the piping of the duckling who had
been left behind, the mother stands still, elongates
herself, and intensifies her incessant guiding call. If
the straggler does not come along and continues to
pipe, then the mother goes racing back towards the
lost duckling—apparently forgetting the ducklings
still following her. When she reaches the straggler,
she voices her greeting and conversation; the newly
found duckling chimes in happily. The young are
content and peaceful until the rest of the ducklings,

who had been with the mother but are now aban-
doned, begin to pipe. As described earlier, they are
psychically incapable of turning in place or moving
at a sharp angle; so they could not follow the mother's hasty return. Their reaction now causes the
mother to repeat her behavior pattern. But the lost
duckling who is now with her, in contrast to the other
group of ducklings, makes an effort to follow her.
This effort is successful for only a few meters, because the mother's usual inhibition against moving
quickly disappears completely in this particular case.
But the duckling does get closer to the first group of
ducklings. The latter group in the meantime have
been 'piping on the spot' long enough to have forgotten the previous line of march. So they are psychically capable of hastening a few meters toward their
mother as she hastens back to them. Thus the two
groups gradually come closer together until they are
finally united in a burst of greeting sounds.

The mournful cry of abandonment among many species
does not seem to be distinct from calls emitted by hungry
or freezing young ducklings. But goslings and cygnets
also have a rest call which the flock uses to establish its
rest period. In this period the small young are warmed by
their mother.

e) The leap of the common murre

Before baby common murres are completely ready for
flight, they suddenly become restless in the evening. They
gravitate toward the edge of the rocky cliff from which
they had shrank before, and their sound-contact call now
sounds like a hoarse squawk. Their parents have only
three days in which to familiarize themselves with this
new call. At this point their personal acquaintance with
their young becomes a vital matter. For at the end of the
third day after this new call was initiated, the young com-

mon murre plunges over the cliff, which may be 100 meters high. As it falls, it beats its wings mightily to brake the velocity of its fall. But all those who fall on the rocks are dashed to bits, and the gleanings are snatched up by ravens and predatory gulls. Only those common murre who land on grass or water survive the leap. As soon as the young common murres make their leap, the adults fly after them and land in the water. Thanks to their calls, parents and children find one another again and swim out to sea together. Tschanz was able to prove that parent and child recognize each other personally in their calls.

f) *Communication in a flock of sparrows*

Until the short brooding period, which runs from April to June, tree sparrows live in flocks or colonies. When the colony sits on a thick hedge, they bombard each other with a whole array of sounds. The sparrows threaten each other and mate, sing softly and then sound a sudden alarm. If the air is clear, they will fly over to a nearby grain field. To synchronize the 100 or more individuals in such a colony, the tree sparrow has three different contact calls at its disposal (Berck, 1961). One is emitted primarily before and during flight takeoff; the second is emitted primarily in flight; and the third is sounded in flight, during the search for food, and before the nest box. Listening to the variations in one call, Gisela Deckert (1962) could tell whether the flight would be short or cover a long distance. We can be quite sure that the birds can also tell this.

g) *Calls from the night sky*

In the late summer and autumn of every year many species of birds leave the temperate zones and spend the period between then and spring in more pleasant zones. In these migrations, many of the long-distance travellers among the small birds travel by night. On such trips many species, which are not seen in swarms otherwise, stick together. Since they cannot see each other at night, sound contact is their only means of maintaining their cohesion. There are a whole series of species that have developed a special call for this purpose. If one plays this call at night to caged members of the same species, they will fly blindly against the roof of the cage—even though they may have already had sad experiences with this behavior pattern (Hamilton, 1962). The drive to join the flight is irresistible for migratory birds. In all likelihood birds in the wild, resting for the moment, are also dragged along by the call of other members of their species as they fly overhead.

h) Begging by young birds

When a young short-toed treecreeper hatches from the egg, it is naked, blind, and helpless. At birth it weighs 0.8 grams. Its manifestations of life are wholly out of tune with its quest to achieve a weight of 8 to 9 grams as quickly as possible, the latter being the weight of an adult treecreeper. To achieve this end the fledgling must eat, and it must also be warmer than its environment. It gets food from its parents, but warmth from its mother alone. In all this the youngster does not do much of an active nature. On the first day it often stretches out of its own accord, raising its neck high and opening its beak. It also responds to the feeding calls of its parents, which are uttered only if the chick does not open up. During the first few days the chick cannot see, but it can induce the parents to provide feedings by emitting a begging call. Most insessorial young make use of this call—burrow brooders more than open-air brooders because the former are relatively safe from enemies.

Haartman (1953) took six of seven young pied flycatchers out of their nest. Since there was now only one chick in the nest, the parents were not as quick to provide frequent feedings. The other six chicks, now hungry, were then brought near the nest so that their parents could hear all seven even though they could see only one. At once the rate of attempted feedings doubled. The one chick in the nest could not handle this glut of food naturally, so the parents ended up eating some of it themselves.

Begging calls are not absolutely necessary for young blackbirds in the course of breeding. A deaf pair of blackbirds brought up several broods in their cage. But these observations of birds in captivity should not be applied to the conditions prevailing in the free world of nature, for the successful rearing in captivity could be explained simply by the much larger supply of food available to the birds.

i) Begging by adults

Since we have just been talking about begging by young birds, let us consider the case of one oscine species at egg-laying time. Our example here is the great tit. At egg-laying time one might think that the young tits had flown the coop. That is what it sounds like in the garden or the woods. If you take a look at the food-hunting pair, you will find the female—recognizable from the fact that the stripe on her chest is less markedly black—sitting on a branch and looking quite worn out. From time to time she emits a begging cry (Fig. 34). If the male comes in her vicinity, she will flutter her wings and move about just as a young bird does. In complete contrast to their usual behavior in winter when great tits are very jealous of their food, as we know from observing their food trays, the male great tit brings the choicest morsels to his partner during the brooding period. What purpose this serves we do not know. It could be a part of the mating process, helping the partners to attune themselves to each other. In addition, it may also be a real food supplement for the female, worn out from laying up to thirteen eggs.

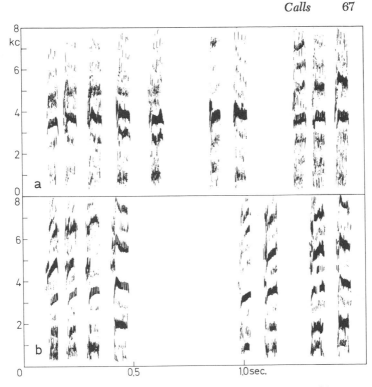

Fig. 34. (*a*) Begging calls of almost fledged great tits. (*b*) Begging call of a female great tit at mating time.

k) *Defense against nest enemies*

The bird's nest does not just attract human beings, it also attracts jays, magpies, squirrels, martens, weasels, mice, and many others. Some of these nest predators, e.g., jays, cannot ordinarily jeopardize burrow brooders. But if a weasel or a mouse appears at the entrance of a brooding tit's burrow, it will be met with an explosive hiss. It is enough to scare a human being, whether or not he is expecting the sound. Most people simply hear the hiss. But if one gets a look into the nest burrow, as Terry Gompertz did (Fig. 35), one can ascertain much.

Fɪɢ. 35.   Brooding great tit in the final phase of a defensive hiss against a nest enemy. (After Gompertz, 1967.)

The whole behavior pattern goes something like this. The tit lays out its feathers, moves it head back so that its beak seems almost to be on top, then opens its beak and lifts it back a little. Suddenly the wings beat against the walls of the burrow and the head comes racing forward. The hiss follows close upon the heels of the noise made by the wings (Fig. 36). In this process the tail is spread quite wide, and the bird falls back into the nest trough. The hiss can be repeated many times.

Here we have a fine example of sound and movement being combined into an impressive behavior pattern. How deeply this impresses a marten or a weasel we do not know. But this behavior pattern is displayed by all tits that have been investigated, and this fact alone bespeaks its value. Hissing shows up frequently in the animal world as a defensive mechanism. But this interplay of hissing and movement is characteristic of tits alone.

Young tits, not yet fledged, already have the hiss at their disposal in the last days of nesting. The early ap-

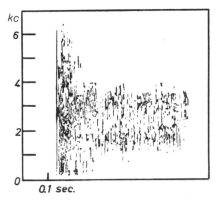

Fig. 36. Sound spectrogram of a hiss coming from a great tit. The first vertical line reproduces the introductory wing flapping. (After Gompertz, 1967.)

pearance of this behavior pattern is highly significant, for only at the beginning of the nesting period does the female normally stay with the young to keep them warm. Later on the adults come only to feed them.

The automaticity of the hissing pattern is evident in the case of hand-reared tits. Even though they may have confidence in the food-providing human being, the right stimulus can provoke a minute-long hiss.

l) *Misleading the enemy*

In the previous section we described how tits defend themselves against nest enemies by scaring them away. Other species have 'hit upon' something else. The egg-lay of ground-breeding birds are especially exposed to many dangers. Their eggs are looked upon as delicacies by many predators: mice, cats, martens, weasels, polecats, foxes, porcupines and, last but not least, human beings. Against some of these predators the bird almost always employs a behavior pattern that seems to be quite refined.

Consider what happens when a fox appears in the vicinity of the Kentish plover's nest. The brooding bird gets up and runs away from the nest as fast as possible, hoping that the fox has not seen it at all. When he is far enough from the nest, he flies towards the predator and drops suddenly in a state of convulsive twitches. He spreads out his wings, makes a conspicuous call, and drags his 'broken wing' limply along the ground (Fig. 37). He then scampers forward like a mouse, only to drop again in a fit of

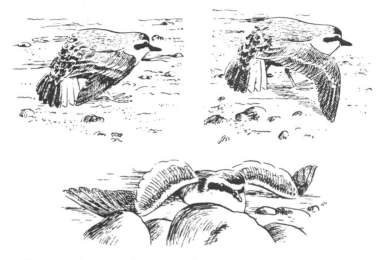

Fig. 37.   A snowy plover misleading an enemy. (After Simmons, 1955.)

sickness. No fox can resist such an easy prey, and he immediately tries to snatch it up. But his prey eludes him just as he is about to grab it. Once the fox has been lured far enough away from the nest by this behavior, the bird bids him 'hail and farewell' and flies back to its nest.

The proverbial cunning of Reynard the Fox breaks down in the face of this transparent ploy, which ornithologists call 'misleading' (*Verleiten*).[1] The little plover seems to be quite clever. To be sure, it is instinct rather

---

1. Translator's note: In the English-speaking world, this behavior is referred to by such terms as 'diversionary' behavior or 'distraction-display' behavior.

than intelligence that is responsible for this behavior. Over the course of hundreds of thousands of years, those plovers who showed the most mastery of this behavior pattern were the ones who had the most fledglings. That is how the pattern developed to the stage of perfection it displays today. We do not know whether the bird's call is decisive in this pattern, or even whether it has any influence on the predator at all. The calls may simply sound the alarm to the bird's mate, or induce the unfledged chick to stay still.

m) Alarm[2]

Apart from song, the most frequently noted bird sounds are those which advertise some potential or actual danger. This is no accident of course, because danger lurks all around the bird and its brood. Therefore alarm calls are very common and can be heard almost anywhere. Furthermore, man himself is treated as a predator, so he has every opportunity to gain practical, firsthand knowledge of how birds react in situations of danger.

Many species make use of a wide range of calls in the presence of predators. Blackbirds have five different calls for this situation: dook, ziep, tix, a flight alarm (Fig. 38), and a distress call.

The first call (Fig. 38 a) indicates a potential danger to the nest. The second call (38 b) is emitted by blackbirds when they are provoked more seriously. The third call (38 c) comes from blackbirds scurrying for cover. The flight alarm (38 d) is primarily directed against dangerous raptors, i.e., hawks and owls. The distress call comes from blackbirds in the clutches of an enemy. Like other calls, the alarm call is not heard in just one situation. Hence the associations indicated here represent a great deal of simplification.

---

2. The sources for this section are summarized in the treatments by Curio (1963) and Thielcke (1970).

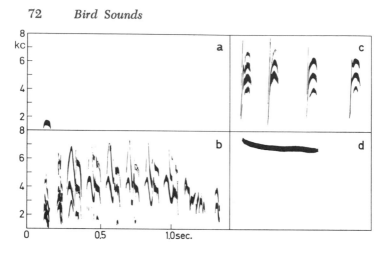

FIG. 38 *a–d.* Alarm calls of the blackbird: (*a*) dook, (*b*) ziep, (*c*) tix, (*d*) flight alarm.

The treecreeper gets by with one call for all the afore-mentioned situations. It is slightly modified only in the fright cry. Many species will actually assault far more powerful enemies in the vicinity of the nest. In so doing they utter special calls or alter their normal cry of alarm to some extent (Fig. 39). Terns can inflict bloody scalp wounds on human beings in the process. The fieldfare

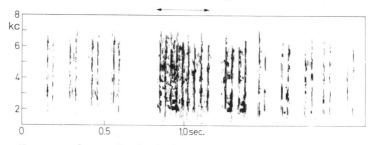

FIG. 39.   Alarm calls of a fieldfare in flight. The bird flies directly at the predator, sprays it with droppings, and then veers off directly over its head. In the section marked by the two-headed arrow, the fieldfare is closest to the enemy. At this time his calls are louder and emitted in quicker succession.

sprays its droppings in the face of a nest predator. I can testify to the effectiveness of these methods from my own experience.

Many species have different calls for ground enemies and flying enemies on the prowl. Carrion crows make for a higher vantage point when they hear the flight alarm. When they have caught sight of a flying goshawk, they fly up high and attack him from above. The goshawk is a threat only when he can drop down on the crow from above. If the goshawk sets down somewhere, the crow also alights some distance away. The crow's flight-alarm call is now replaced by his ground alarm. He keeps his eyes fixed on the goshawk, uttering a deafening cry when the goshawk moves even the slightest bit.

This mobbing behavior is widespread among the oscines, to which social corvids also belong. The mere appearance of an owl in the daytime will soon cause him to be surrounded by a swarm of noisy blackbirds, chaffinches, and tits. Raising a hue and cry, they circle the predator at a distance and attract more and more birds.

In areas where the pygmy owl is present, one need only imitate its melodious whistle to attract a swarm of coal tits, chaffinches, and treecreepers—all shouting their cry of alarm. Many opinions have been voiced about the purport of this mobbing behavior. In all likelihood it serves to make birds acquainted with their enemy; and it may also serve to point out his favorite resting place. Birds have an excellent memory for places where they have had unpleasant experiences.

The pygmy owl hunts in the daytime. His chief prey are small birds. It is particularly important for the latter to know at all times where their enemy dwells. Once the enemy is known and recognized, he can scarcely be dangerous anymore. So in areas inhabited by the pygmy owl, the small birds have trained themselves to recognize its call. The resourceful ornithologist puts this fact to good use. Playing imitations of the pygmy owl to small birds, he can establish from the reaction of the latter whether the pygmy owl is present in a given locality.

Ground predators usually trigger the same alarm calls that perched owls do. Crows also display their mobbing behavior toward a perched goshawk. Small birds also utter their flight alarm from cover when they see a flying sparrow hawk. When they are greatly excited, they also use it to point out a perched sparrow hawk. As soon as other birds hear this call, they 'freeze'. That is, they sit tight and motionless if they are in a safe place, or they scurry for cover if they are not in a safe place.

Just as crows display mobbing behavior for the goshawk, so barn swallows do toward their chief enemy, the hobby—here again in flight. Before they do, however, they must get beyond the hobby. Otherwise they are usually lost. From the call of the barn swallow, specialists can tell whether their mobbing is directed at a hobby or a sparrow hawk. Unlike the hobby, the sparrow hawk is not an enemy to be taken very seriously by the barn swallow. Turkey hens use different calls to point out a high-flying buzzard and a low-flying one. These are examples to show that many species use several calls to make fine distinctions between different situations. We can be fairly certain that the birds grasp these nuances just as well as we do.

Inexperienced chicks of the domestic fowl react like grownups to the flight alarm of the latter. Even while still in the egg, they will shut up when they hear it. Newly hatched golden pheasants will scatter in every direction as soon as they hear their mother's warning, even though they are very shaky on their feet otherwise. Capercaillie chicks reared without a mother, who had never seen a flying enemy before, scanned the sky when they heard an imitation of the flight alarm.

Altricial birds, i.e., species which, unlike precocial birds, are cared for by their parents in the nest for some time after hatching, shut up in the nest and sink lower into it when their parents sound the alarm. If the youngsters are pretty far along in their development, steadily continuing alarm calls can induce them to leave their nest. They are particularly sensitive to the fright cry of a brother or sister bird; it instantaneously drives them from the nest in all directions. By this means they ensure that not all of them will become the predator's prey. For they are much safer from even the sharpest eyes when they are pressed down close to the ground.

Using fright cries, one can drive even grown ravens from their sleeping place, and sparrows from their night-time burrows. Red-backed shrikes, who have just left home and are sitting in contact with each other, will start up at once when they hear the alarm call of their species. Then they will 'freeze', or plunge blindly to the ground, flatten themselves, and lie motionless (Fig. 40). White-throats and chiffchaffs use special calls to their youngsters who have left home, in order to lure them out of a danger zone.

In figure 38 we examined the flight alarm of a black-bird. Marler (1956) compared this call among different species and ascertained interesting correspondences. Even though blackbirds, great tits, and reed buntings are not

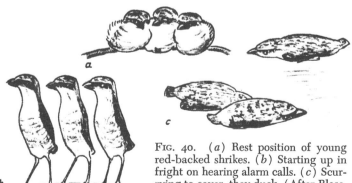

FIG. 40. (*a*) Rest position of young red-backed shrikes. (*b*) Starting up in fright on hearing alarm calls. (*c*) Scurrying to cover, they duck. (After Blase, 1960.)

closely related, one cannot distinguish their flight-alarm calls from each other (Fig. 41). This runs counter to our earlier assertion that bird sounds are peculiar to a given species. In this case they are not, and there are special reasons for this. All the flight alarms depicted in figure 41 are very high and long drawn out. They begin and end softly, remain at approximately the same pitch, and are repeated irregularly at great intervals. Most of these characteristics make it difficult to pinpoint the location of a sound source, and Marler took this to be the reason for the correspondences among the different species.

The effect of this particular call upon a human being is startling. Even when it comes from a bird you are holding in your own hand, you have the impression that the sound is coming from anywhere but this bird. But we do not really know whether the sparrow hawk hunts acoustically. The similar structure of alarm calls could also result from some sort of mutual assimilation designed to extend com-

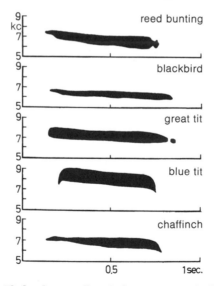

FIG. 41.   Flight-alarm calls of five species. (After Marler in Thorpe, 1961.)

munication beyond the limits of one's own species. But why that should result in a sound that is hard to locate cannot be explained by the hypothesis that communication among the small birds is the determining factor here. While the protection of the caller may be ensured by a sound that is hard to locate, the long-tailed tit has achieved the same result with another tack. The call of the single bird is very easy to locate, but long-tailed tits spend almost the whole year in colonies. When some real threat exists, usually several birds will emit a call (Fig. 42). This makes it hard for the predator to concentrate on one victim.

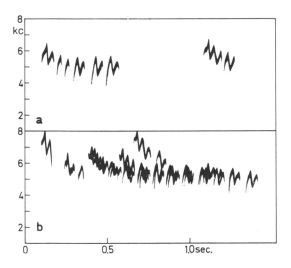

FIG. 42. (*a*) Flight-alarm calls of a long-tailed tit. (*b*) Flight-alarm calls of at least four long-tailed tits simultaneously.

The elimination of species specificity is not so extensive in the case of calls directed against ground enemies and owls. The species can almost always be identified in these calls without too much trouble, even though many but not all small birds are basically similar here (Figs. 43, 78). Ground-alarm calls extend over a wide pitch range, are short, and are rhythmically repeated. In this case the caller can afford to emit a call that is easy to locate, for he is not immediately in jeopardy once he recognizes the danger (Marler, 1957). Indeed there seems to be an advantage in raising a chorus of like-minded callers, so that the enemy will have a hard time. And the sooner this is done, the better. Otherwise the mobbing behavior of small birds would scarcely drive away owls that sleep in the daytime.

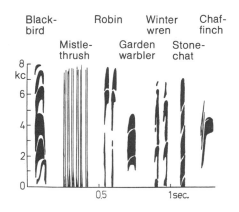

FIG. 43.   Ground alarm calls of seven species. (After Marler in Thorpe, 1961.)

The frequency with which birds sound an alarm is primarily dependent on the time of year and the concurrent stage of the brooding cycle. When their young are ready to fly off on their own, their parents will react almost hysterically to the slightest disturbance that never bothered them before. The closer an enemy is to the nest, the more adult birds will sound the alarm. The fright cry of a seized bird will attract all the members of the species around and prompt attacks on the predator. Perhaps the main value of the adult's reaction is that it diverts the enemy from the nest. Jackdaws, who live in colonies, will rasp in unison if you pick up a fledged chick. In fact a jackdaw with a black feather in its beak will trigger the same rasping. This fact indicates how undiscerningly the pattern operates.

n) *The sound store of the treecreeper*

Besides song, our two species of treecreeper have more than ten different calls in their repertoire. Here we intend to take a closer look at eight of these calls, since their social import is quite well known.

If a male comes singing into the territory of another pair, he is answered by a series of calls in quick succession (Fig. 44 a, b). These make it quite clear to the intruder that this section of wood is already occupied. Only someone who is really acquainted with treecreepers hears these sounds. Those of the short-toed treecreeper sound like a pale version of the blackbird's tix sound (Fig. 38 c). It is probably quite clear to a male treecreeper, for it is only used against rivals.

If we observe the treecreeper's nest at the beginning of the brooding period, we will see the female leaving the clutch. This gives rise solely to the delicate contact calls one can hear whenever a treecreeper changes its habitat (Fig. 44 g, h). At the end of the brooding period treecreepers become more and more excited by this stimulus. The resultant calls are short and spaced far apart; those of the short-toed treecreeper sound like a tüt. By the end of the nestling period, young treecreepers are already in command of this alarm call. A very similar call can be heard in intra-species conflicts between two males; but in this case the call is more variable and uttered in quick succession (Fig. 44 c, d).

If you grab a fledged young bird out of the nest, it will emit a shrill call. Upon hearing it, all the young will try to abandon the nest. Adult treecreepers also utter the fright cry when they are seized (Fig. 44 e, f). *Certhia familiaris* does this more frequently than *Certhia brachdactyla,* but we do not know why.

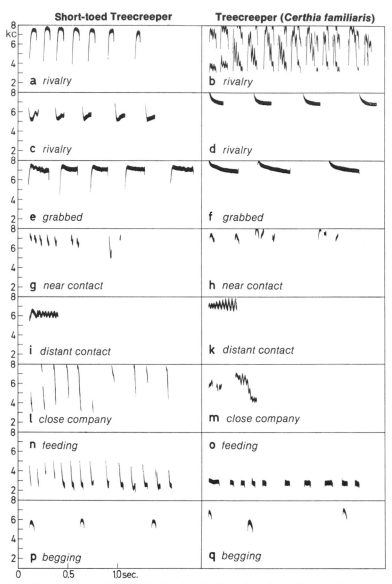

FIG. 44 *a–q.* Calls of *Certhia brachydactyla* and *Certhia familiaris*. The close-company calls of the latter are from young birds (juveniles). The begging calls of the latter are from two nestlings.

Two sound-contact calls serve to keep the pair together, one when they are near each other (Fig. 44 g, h) and one when they are far away from each other (Fig. 44 i, k). The distant-contact call is also the begging call of older youngsters for food. At mating time it serves both male and female as a call for food.

Treecreepers are territorial the whole year round. In other words, males advertise their territory to rivals throughout the year. This rule is broken in the winter, however, for on cold winter nights neighboring pairs will sleep in close feather contact (Fig. 45). In areas where dense swarms of treecreepers dwell, such as public parks with many old oak trees, as many as twenty pairs may sleep together. In this case they will emit a sleeping-quarters call not heard otherwise (Fig. 44 l, m), probably to overcome their mutual antipathy. Young treecreepers who have flown away from the nest also sleep in contact. It must get pretty cold before *Certhia familiaris* overcomes its dread of coming in close contact with a companion. In the aviary it took a temperature of minus 14° C. *Certhia familiaris* is apparently quite well adapted to cold, for it spends the winter in the Arctic darkness of Scandinavia.

Parent treecreepers use special calls to get their youngsters to open up (Fig. 44 n, o). These calls are sounded only in this situation. They are so soft that they can only be heard by someone standing in the immediate vicinity. The begging calls of the youngster changes continually as it grows older. We shall return to this point later. Figure 44 (p, q) depicts the begging calls of young treecreepers in the first two days of their lives.

This overview is incomplete and greatly oversimplified. There are a whole series of soft calls that I have not yet recorded on tape because they are heard only rarely. And there are other calls that I have not yet been able to classify satisfactorily in terms of function. Even this incomplete presentation would not have been possible without extensive observations in the field. But in any case the

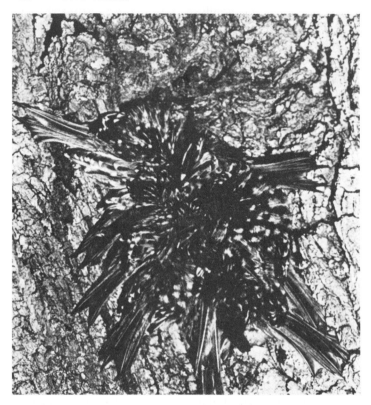

FIG. 45.   Short-toed treecreepers sleeping in feather contact in the winter time. In the photo one can glimpse 9 out of approximately 15 individuals. (After Löhrl, 1955.)

main point of my studies was not to provide a functional classification of the individual calls, as subsequent sections should make clear.

o) Summary

In contrast to bird song, which is far more striking and conspicuous, bird calls have so far been given little attention by scientists. This is quite unjustified, as I have tried to show in this chapter. In many cases we know little or nothing about the significance of many calls in the social life of a pair or a group. To probe the meaning of calls, we must first of all catalogue the situations in which they are heard. In many cases we are not yet beyond that first step. But even at this stage the following summary may help to suggest the manifold possibilities of avian vocal communication.

Intercourse with members of the same species requires not only peaceful behavior but often very specific behavior. Thus threatening gestures and calls are part and parcel of the everyday social life of birds. The aggressive intent of such threatening can vary greatly. At one end of the scale, sounds and movements amount to attack. At the other end of the scale, they are signs of meekness that appease the attacker. Pain caused by a member of the same species can likewise be answered with a specific call.

There are many different vocal ways of pinpointing, chasing, and decoying a predator. We have discussed them in detail in the section on alarm (m).

Many behavior patterns have been developed to keep the avian pair together and to attune them to each other. This synchronization is necessary so that both partners will be ready at the same time to build their nest, to copulate, and to brood, feed, and care for their young. Here again the bird's vocabulary is rich and varied. Special calls serve to keep the pair together, to greet one another, to alternate brooding shifts, and to convey food to the young. Species which sleep in feather contact have calls for signalling close company. Synchronization also seems to be furthered by mating calls, begging calls, nest-indication calls, and copulation calls.

Outside of the brooding period many avian species stick together in more or less tightly knit colonies. Special calls before takeoff, during flight, and before landing indicate that the members of the colony are well informed about each other's intentions. Thus they can attune their actions to each other accordingly. Of particular significance are the calls to be heard from migratory birds at night. Some species have calls to direct members of the species to a food source.

Many precocial chicks use calls to synchronize their hatching. They also use calls to make their discomfort known to their parents and to signal cold, hunger, pain, or abandonment. We do not yet know whether the parents can recognize these needs, which call for four very different behavioral reactions, solely from the calls of their fledglings. Precocial young and nidifugous birds who have left the nest maintain sound contact with their parents and each other, thus ensuring that they will stick together or be found again. Rest calls and close-company calls complete the repertoire of young birds. They in turn are stimulated, fed, prodded, and guided by calls from their parents.

Special use of calls is made by the oilbird, related to our nightjar, and by the swiftlet of southern Asia. They build their nests in the dark recesses of rocky caves where eyesight can offer no orientation. Like the bat, whose approach is known to us, they use the echo of their own calls to find the right way in the dark. This is a perfect example of how similar external conditions lead to the same solution among different groups of animals.

In many cases it is not easy to determine the import of a call. Consider the short-toed treecreeper. It will utter its tüt call both as a flight alarm and as a ground alarm if a foreign member of the species appears in his territory or at its border, or after an altercation with a rival. A distinction is still possible to the extent that alarm calls are less variable and come in slower succession. The rivalry calls, which vary more, can be slower or faster; they can also be combined with other calls (Fig. 82).

In many cases wholly different calls flow into one another. In fact calls can easily flow over into song (Fig. 46). We do not know for sure whether mixed forms of two calls take on a new meaning. Such mixed calls may

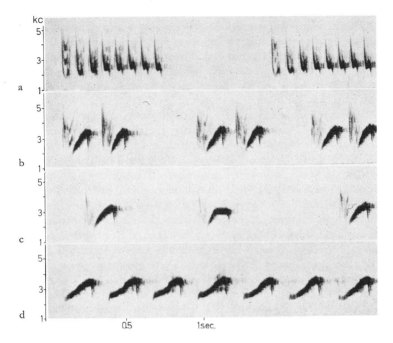

Fig. 46.   Rivalry calls of the nuthatch (*a–c*) gradually shifting into its song (*d*). The stimulus was a nuthatch song. His first response was short and quick (*a*). It then became longer and slower (*b, c*). The single call in (*c*) differs very little from a song element in (*d*). The four spectrograms are sections of a longer sound series.

only be an external indication of the bird shifting from one mood to another. Or they may indicate that the calls which are intermingled now go back to one and the same source. In other words, they may both have arisen from one call hundreds of thousands of years ago. Much more work will have to be done before we can reach any sure conclusion on this matter.

IX. *Learning*

a) *Mimicry*

If you listen to a starling singing, you may be in for a few surprises. He may flap his wings and imitate a lip-smacking kiss, or suddenly cackle like a hen, or sing like a cuckoo for a moment, or whistle like an oriole. The original and the imitation cannot be distinguished from each other. This behavior would seem to contradict the point I stressed earlier, i.e., that one can readily recognize any species from its sounds.

Nature has built in safeguards, however, to make sure that everyone cannot sing everything. The imitation section of an avian song usually makes up a small portion of its repertoire, and in many cases only fragments of another species' song are imitated (Fig. 47). Furthermore, the imitations may distort the original timbre. The fact is that males of the species being imitated react very weakly to full blown imitations when they are built into the song of the imitator species. But they do react pretty strongly in the exceptional case where their strophe is uttered alone by some imitator, or when it is played by itself on a tape recorder (Tretzel, 1965 a, 1967).

The mimetic imitation of many avian species attracted the attention of ornithologists in earlier centuries, causing them to wonder which portions of song are innate and which must be learned. Ferdinand von Pernau was way ahead of his time in doing research on this question at the beginning of the eighteenth century. But it is only in re-

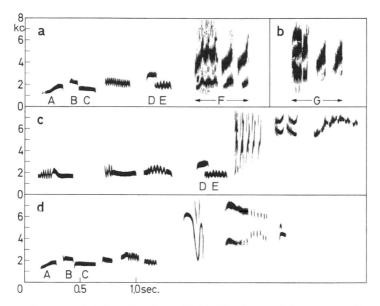

Fig. 47. (*a*) Strophe of a wild blackbird, recorded in 1960, (*b*) alarm call of a pekin robin, (*c, d*) two strophes of the same male blackbird, recorded in 1959. In 1960 the blackbird (*F*) imitated the call of the pekin robin (*G*). In 1959 elements of strophe (*a*) are combined differently (*c, d*), and the imitation of the pekin robin is absent.

cent decades, with the aid of tape recorders and sound spectrographs, that it has become possible to explore this problem with any chance of success. After World War II the whole problem was tackled anew by the Dane, H. Poulsen (1951), the Englishman, W. H. Thorpe (1954), and the German, O. Koehler (1951).

b) *Innate and learned*

The ability to reproduce something one has heard is basically restricted to song birds, humming birds, parrots, and human beings. A chicken cannot imitate sounds any more than a dog can. Only about 0.4 percent of all animal species can learn in this way. Within this group a sharp distinction is made between the capacity to imitate one's own species and the capacity to imitate other species. Whether this is justified is a moot point.

By 'innate' in this context we mean only that which a bird can produce without an acoustic model but with the use of self-control over his hearing. Here everything else will be called 'learned'. What takes place when self-control is ruled out is something we shall treat in the chapter on juvenile development (13).

Experiments and studies about the role of innate and learned factors are not simple. But they are particularly difficult in the realm of acoustics. The first presupposition is that the bird will be shielded from the surrounding environment, but even the erection of a soundproof room presents a great problem. Walls are not a great problem; neither are doors and windows. But a bird needs air as well. How are we to let air into the room without undermining the soundproofing? It is a very difficult problem to solve without getting stuck with exorbitant outlays of energy and money. When one is not able to make a whole load of experiments, one can only change one factor of unknown effect in each experiment; otherwise one will reach false interpretations of the results.

If you isolate a single song bird one week after hatching, however, you are depriving it of much more than its acoustic surroundings. Under natural conditions it grows up with its brothers and sisters. And even after it is fledged, it stays with them in many cases—playing, hunting, threatening, preening, etc. So we must be careful to rule out the possibility that something in all this is significant for the formation of vocalizations by comparing birds raised in a group with the bird raised alone. We must also play records of the whole song repertoire of birds living in the wild to the single bird raised in isolation. When a bird has been subjected to this range of sounds and develops a normal song, we have made a good deal of progress. For it is now easy to explain differences between its song and that of an isolated male who was not allowed to hear anything. The 'imperfect' song of the latter must be due to the fact that we cut off its possibilities for learning.

Unlike the case of chickens and other avian species that are not very demanding, the artificial rearing of young song birds from the egg on has not been a very successful endeavor. Under the harsh requirements imposed by the matter of soundproofing, only F. Sauer and the Messmers have managed it. Early isolation itself is very important when we consider that three-day-old blackbird chicks can be trained in a melody. E. and I. Messmer (1956) merely had to whistle to them in a certain way when they fed them. In short order the blackbirds would open up as soon as they heard the first sounds. And it should be pointed out that a three-day-old blackbird chick is naked and blind.

We do not know if a blackbird chick can retain something it heard so early in life. We know for sure that it cannot imitate it exactly later on. But can it imitate it to a degree? In any event there is the case of one species, the Oregon junco, where isolated song was 'improved' by offering it a large repertoire of sounds even though specific elements were not imitated. This did not take place at a very early stage in the life of the bird being investigated. But the very early 'imprinting' of a specific strophe of the feeding parent may leave its mark on the later song of the offspring.

The white-crowned sparrow.—After this brief introduction

to the problem, we shall begin by considering the white-crowned sparrow of North America. A male of this species has only one strophe, which he reiterates in a very stereotyped fashion. Neighboring males have a very similar song; more distant males show differences in their song (Fig. 59). As we shall see in more detail in the section on dialects, birds in the wild and hand-raised nestlings show great differences in their song (Fig. 60). The last part of Kaspar Hauser strophes, in particular, are imperfect and incomplete.[1] Only *one* male raised alone in isolation injected fairly 'normal' elements into the second part of his strophe, but these elements were not divided into groups. Several males raised together to develop fairly concordant strophes to some extent, but the approximation is not as good as that between wild birds from one dialect area. Thus far, it does not seem that the strophe of a male raised in isolation with others is any more similar to the song of the wild bird than is the strophe of a male raised in total isolation.

The chaffinch.—Chaffinches divide their strophes sharply into phrases (Fig. 48). Each phrase consists of very homogeneous elements, which are qualitatively different from those of the other phrases. The strophe ends with a flourish, which can be composed of several dissimilar elements. In line with the different phrases, the strophe usually drops by stages in pitch as it moves from start to finish. Chaffinches raised singly in isolation usually lack the final flourish and the division of their strophe into phrases, although the final element may stand out a bit from the others. Its elements resemble the simplest elements of the wild bird. Complicated structures are completely absent

---

1. Kaspar Hauser animals are animals raised in isolation from members of their species. The name comes from a young man who ostensibly spent his early years without coming into close contact with human beings. Kaspar Hauser strophes are those of birds raised in auditory isolation.

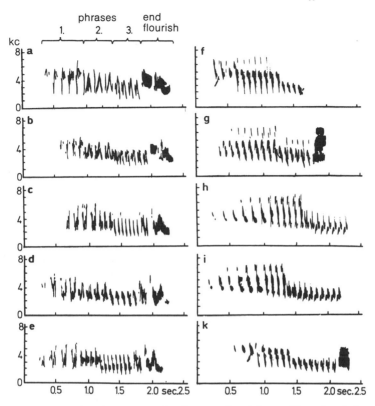

FIG. 48. (*a–e*) One strophe from each of five wild male chaffinches. (*f–k*) One strophe from each of five male chaffinches raised as a group in acoustic isolation. (After Thorpe, 1958).

in the song of the isolated bird (Fig. 49). Chaffinches raised in a group sing 'better' strophes (Fig. 48). The final flourish and the division into phrases are much more marked than in the song of the bird raised by itself alone (Thorpe, 1954).

The blackbird.—The blackbird's song is very rich in variations. The individual elements of its strophe are clearly structured. Simple, straightforward tone bands (Fig. 50 a) are regularly accompanied by rapid fluctuations in pitch. The latter show up as zigzag lines on the spectrogram, e.g., in the middle of element (b) of figure 50. The beginning and end of this element sound somewhat rushed and compressed, and here the pitch band appears to be unravelled—but in a very regular form. The soft-sounding latter portion of the strophe, in particular, may look like an artistic ornament (Fig. 50 c). Great jumps in pitch are the rule here.

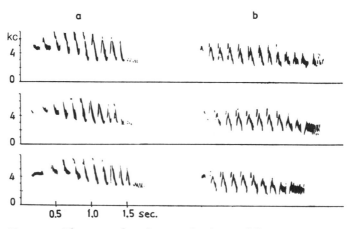

FIG. 49.   Three strophes from each of two different male chaffinches (*a* and *b*), who were raised alone in isolation. (After Thorpe in Nottebohm, 1967.)

A male blackbird raised by himself in isolation is also capable of producing long drawn out tones. Comparatively speaking, in fact, they are often too long (Fig. 50 d). Their structure is frequently deformed, in which case they sound impure and out of tune. In contrast to compressed elements of the wild bird's song, the impurity of tone here is not regular in form (Fig. 50 k). Occasionally the whole strophe consists of uniform elements in sequence (e.g., Fig. 50 g, h, and i). A Kaspar Hauser bird

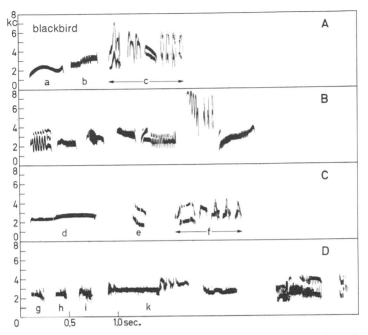

FIG. 50. (A, B) Two strophes of a wild male blackbird. (C, D) Two strophes of a solitary male raised in acoustic isolation. (After tape recordings by E. and I. Messmer, 1956.)

can only produce a vague suggestion (f) of the wild bird's concluding flourish (c). The great range of tones and the structural clarity of the elements is missing. We cannot determine on objective grounds whether the blackbird has more innate song components than the chaffinch, or whether the reverse is true. Both must learn more in order to be able to sing like birds in the wild (E. and I. Messmer; H. and G. Thielcke, 1960).

Juncos.—The juncos of North America (*Junco phaeonotus* and *Junco oreganus*), which belong to the Fringillidae, are closely related to each other. The strophes of *oreganus* are simple, while those of *phaeonotus* are complicated. Just the opposite is true in the case of Kaspar Hauser birds. Birds raised in group isolation come close to the song of wild birds in the case of both species (Marler, 1967).

Summary.—Kaspar Hauser experiments have shown that young song birds learn from older members of their species in order to be able to produce wild song completely and perfectly. It seems that the American song sparrow needs to learn the least even though it has quite a complicated song and a rich repertoire (Mulligan, 1966). The white-crowned sparrow, by contrast, must take over a great deal from older members of its species even though its wild strophe is simple.

Kaspar Hauser song can be simpler or more complicated than wild song, the latter differing even in two closely related species. Among some avian species, the song of males hand-raised as a group develops in closer approximation to wild song than does the song of single individuals hand-raised in isolation. We do not know how this takes place, but it seems justifiable to conclude that a young male of the species 'knows' more about the song to be learned than he can produce alone. Up to now we cannot say for sure whether he has a conception of the complete wild song as well. Knowledge of how the wild song should look must be at least good enough to account for the fact that the song of Group Hauser birds can resemble wild song.[2] That would suffice to keep young males from straying away from the species pattern during their development out in the open.

The latitude within which something can be learned is undoubtedly innate, but there is greater or lesser range

2. Group Hauser birds in this case are several birds of about the same age who have been raised in auditory isolation from the outside world.

within it. If the range is great, additional safeguards may be necessary to ensure that not too many birds deviate sharply from the norm. Otherwise the effectiveness of the song as a signal would be impaired. The tendency to approximate other members of the species in one's song could be that kind of safeguard. We know this effect from laboratory experiments on different species—the chaffinch, the white-crowned sparrow, and two species of tree-creeper (*Certhia brachydactyla* and *Certhia familiaris*)— and also from observations in the wild, for only in this way can dialects arise.

Many species have taken a different tack to maintain the species specificity of their song despite their learning. Among them learning is bound up with a living being with whom they have a 'personal' relationship. These remarkable relationships were first discovered under abnormal conditions, e.g., when the young is reared by a human being or a different species.

Bullfinch and zebra finch.—For a long time bird fanciers have been giving thorough training to bullfinches, whistling a specific tune to them over and over again until the young birds grow weary of hearing it. Intelligent pupils eventually take this sort of strophe into their permanent repertoire. Many bird fanciers find it very pretty; musically inclined neighbors may not. Nicolai (1959) went on from there to raise a male for an even longer period of time. Its son and grandson did not sing like normal bullfinches but rather like their forefather. Thus something alien to the species was transmitted from one generation to the next through the learning process. The decisive factor here was not the species-specific factor, but rather the fact that the food-provider sang. Out in the open bullfinches do not whistle human melodies and young male bullfinches are raised by adult bullfinches, hence the transmission of song with all its features is ensured.

According to the investigations of Immelmann (1967), zebra finches behave in the same manner. One surprising fact is that the song of both bullfinches and zebra finches serves primarily to stimulate their mates; it does not serve to mark out a territory. Such a firm learning tie to paternal song is not to be expected among birds with dialects.

c) Sensitive phases

A particular form of learning is called 'imprinting' by behavioral scientists. Animals are open to imprinting only during a specific phase of their life. Another characteristic of imprinting is that things learned in this way are never forgotten later.

The ability to learn song begins around the thirtieth day of life in song birds. In zebra finches, which are very precocious, it appears even before the twenty-fifth day. Do they retain nothing of what they have heard prior to this time? We do not know the answer to that question, but total loss seems quite doubtful when we realize that three-day-old blackbirds can already distinguish a feeding melody from another melody. Perhaps at this early stage they notice only general, basic features of song without being able to detect specific structures by comparing what they have heard with what they themselves produce. This type of learning does actually show up in somewhat older juncos (Marler, 1967). When birds raised in isolation are offered the wild song of their species, they do improve the structure of their own strophes. But one will look in vain for specific learned elements in their song.

When we say that a given species begins its learning at a given point in time, we are talking here about learning that is detectable to our hearing and evident on a sound spectrogram; up to now only this has been investigated in connection with the onset of the sensitive phase. Immelmann (1967) has shown that with the onset of the sensitive phase a bird's learning capacity improves as it grows older.

White-crowned sparrows appear to be open to imprinting from the song of their species only in the period which runs from the thirtieth to the hundredth day of life. The onset may be somewhat earlier. Chaffinches learn a whole lot of wild song during their first summer, but only in the following spring do they take over the fine details of dialect. Their strophes are fixed after their thirteenth month. The crucial point here is that the bird has gone through a process of development which ends provisionally with strophes uttered in a stereotyped fashion. If we block this development artificially by castrating the male, the capacity for learning is maintained. A castrated male does not sing because he lacks testosterone, the male sex hormone. Nottebohm (1967) implanted testosterone in a two-year-old chaffinch who had been castrated at an early age. He then played two normal chaffinch strophes to the bird, who learned them despite his 'old' age.

The learning readiness of the blackbird starts around the twenty-eighth day and extends to the hundredth day (at the very least). It is very probable that they are also receptive during the autumn. We have demonstrated learning capacity during the following winter and early spring in hand-raised males. But even wild blackbirds are capable of learning more in later years. This we determined with a banded male who could be recognized individually. Our helper in this case was the pekin robin. In 1958 a colleague had found one pekin robin who had apparently flown away from some bird lover. We bought a mate for it, kept the two in isolation at first, and then transferred them to the aviary. During this period our male blackbird could hear them every day. He was at least four years old at the time. The year after next he produced astonishing imitations of the pekin robin's impressive alarm call (Fig. 47), which he almost certainly had not heard before he was five years old. In 1959 the other elements (A, B, C, and D, E) had appeared in different combinations, as strophes (c) and (d) indicate.

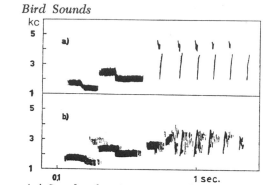

Fig. 51. (*a*) Strophe of an American wood thrush; in March it was played twelve times in quick succession to a blackbird who had been hand-raised in isolation the previous year. (*b*) The same strophe imitated by this blackbird.

d) *How often must a bird hear something to learn it?*

We played the strophe of an American wood thrush twelve times to a blackbird in March of the latter's first year. The blackbird imitated this strophe quite well (Fig. 51). But far more astonishing is the learning readiness of young song birds at a period when they themselves do not yet sing, or when they can only produce a soft, twittering juvenile song. At this stage blackbirds will occasionally try to imitate a sound model right after hearing it. Now and then they succeed to a degree, but these attempts are quite poor in comparison with later ones.

e) *Situational use of learned calls*

If you approach the nest of a great tit, you may on occasion hear the alarm call of the coal tit, the short-toed treecreeper, or the song thrush. At first you are inclined to doubt your own powers of recollection, because you thought you had been keeping watch over a great tit's nest. You look up and feel reassured. For there is your great tit—emitting the coal tit's call. Alarm calls of other species are apparently very well suited for use in an appropriate situation. On the whole, however, such instances are not too frequent.

In captivity African gray parrots learn to speak quite often. This can go far beyond mere mechanical repetition. The parrots may use specific human words in a meaningful way, or else use a word of their own devising to demand the fulfillment of a particular request. Take the case of Koehler (1951), whose parrot called 'kuducks' every evening until his cage was covered with a cloth. It was a particularly bad scene when no one was home to cater to his wish, for his loud cry soon induced Koehler's neighbors to make nasty calls of their own.

f) Ravens call their partners by names

Many raven calls are very plastic. This is rare among birds, whose calls are usually quite fixed and inflexible. Their songs, on the other hand, can frequently be changed by learning. In captivity the talented raven learns a wide variety of sounds: a turkey's gobble, a stork's clatter, a dog's bark, a man's cough, a few human words. The imitations are so perfect that you can immediately recognize the original source.

In time every raven collects a repertoire which distinguishes it from every other raven—even from its mate, with which it remains permanently. As soon as the male and female of a pair are separated, each begins to call the other with the other's own repertoire (Gwinner, 1962). Both then try to get back together as soon as possible. Kneutgen's shama birds from India behaved exactly the same way. Both ravens and shamas 'designate' their partners by name, using calls that are characteristic of the partner alone. We are led to conclude that this behavior also serves to keep the pair together in the wild.

Löhrl (1968) observed this kind of 'name-designating' behavior among jays in the wild. Like all the members of the crow family, jays are inclined toward all sorts of behavior we would consider as practical joking. Every morning these particular jays, living in their favorite park in Ludwigsburg, inspected different burrows of the tawny owl and lambasted the occupants with abusive language. We have already mentioned this general type of 'mobbing behavior' in chapter 8 (section m). Löhrl wanted to know what would happen if no owl were in the burrow. So he snatched one owl and held it in captivity for a couple of days. The jays came the next morning as usual, and started their tirade. But they became dead silent as soon as they took a peek into the burrow. For there in front of them was a big, life-like, stuffed owl. The specimen attracted blackbirds first, and their cries brought more alarmed jays. Before the villification concert, however, two different jays sang like a tawny owl. Hence they recognized their dubious neighbor in the stuffed owl and called him by name.

g) *Is the song thrush a con man?*

The song thrushes flying uncaged in our house developed a curious behavior pattern. At first they used to utter their high alarm call 'ziii', quite appropriately when a bird outside flew close by the window. All the inhabitants of the room—fieldfares, blackbirds, and song thrushes—immediately rushed for cover. Later on, the song thrushes also uttered their flight alarm when one of the stronger fieldfares or blackbirds snatched a morsel of food away from them. Still later, they started their warning cry as soon as we put their dinner of worms on the food dish. This behavior was very much to the advantage of the alarm-sounding song thrushes, who were able to gobble down a few worms while the other birds headed for cover or froze for a few moments. To a human observer it looked like the cute trick of a con man.

But we must be careful about imposing our notions of morality on animal behavior. For it seems unlikely that the song thrushes had any insight into their own behavior. The alarm calls themselves were not confined solely to one situation. At the start the song thrushes may have sounded the call to air the oppression they were suffering at the hands of stronger birds. The success of this 'unintentional' reaction then led to more frequent use of the call. The song thrushes themselves showed us how little judgment was involved in the use of this pattern. For on occasion they themselves were swept along into retreat by the echoing alarm calls of the fleeing blackbirds and field-fares. So they failed to profit from their 'trickery'.

h) Dialects

If an American tries to converse with a cockney Lon-doner, he will probably run into problems of understand-ing. Most people realize that the blame is to be put on the difference in dialects. But the noninitiate may be sur-prised to learn that a similar phenomenon occurs among birds.

The chaffinch and his warbling song are widely known. If we listen to a male chaffinch on a bright day in May, we can count off many hundreds of strophes. And his im-mediate neighbors will be just as voluble in their singing. But as we walk along, that particular song will suddenly die out. Now all the chaffinches will be singing a monot-onous 'huid' (Fig. 52 c). It is quite similar to the call used by the redstart to point out a cat. Disappointed by this turn of events, we cross an open field and soon end up in another woods. No chaffinches seem to be present here, for we cannot hear the first song nor the 'huid'. But sud-denly we see a chaffinch right in front of us—only this one is uttering a different sound. Ornithologists say he is 'rülschting' (Fig. 52 f). Once we have become attuned to this sound, we can hear it all around us. For that is the call of all the chaffinches in this particular area.

The fact is that when we crossed the open field, we moved from one chaffinch dialect area to another. The treeless meadow about 400 meters wide contains no chaf-finches; it is large enough to create a sharp boundary be-tween two different dialects. Any small meadow, or any other area that is uninhabitable for a chaffinch, can form

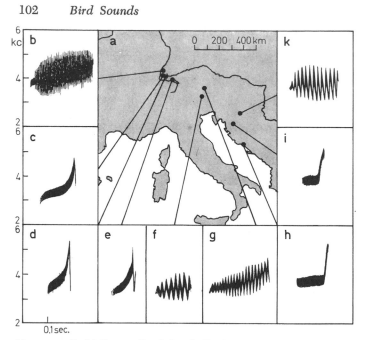

FIG. 52.   (*b–k*) Rain calls of the chaffinch, connected by lines with the places where they were recorded (*a*).

such a boundary. By the same token, the dialect boundary line can also run right through the middle of a forest, in which case the shift is not so abrupt. A male in such a mixed zone may have both calls at his disposal, or he may combine them into some intermediate form.

Besides the 'huid' sound and the 'rülschen' sound, there are a whole series of additional dialects. Ornithologists label them 'rain calls', but we do not really know whether they are uttered more frequently under specific weather conditions. Their social import is probably akin to that of song. Since they are readily distinguishable to our ears, they were known before the sound spectrogram existed. H. Sick reported on them back in 1939.

If we chart the rain-call dialects of many different areas, we will end up with a mosaic-like pattern (Fig. 53). The

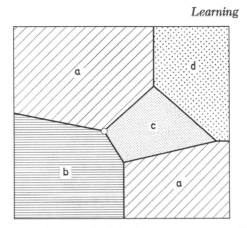

FIG. 53.   Mosaic-like spread of dialects on a diagram. Dialect (*a*) appears in two areas; in the intervening area another dialect (*c*) prevails. If a chaffinch is born at the point where three dialects intersect (*o*), it is equally probable that he will settle down in dialect area (*a*), (*b*), or (*c*).

same dialect can show up in different areas, which are separated by regions with different dialects. Around Freiburg, the Black Forest, and the Lake of Constance, chaffinches have a 'huid' call similar to that of the redstart (Fig. 52 c, d, e). In the Alps they 'rülschen' (f, g). On the coast of Yugoslavia their rain call is again very similar to the 'huid' sound (h, i). If one were to take a complete inventory, one would probably find more dialects. The individual blocks in our mosaic pattern would become smaller, but the principle would remain the same.

The rain calls of the chaffinch are the only calls that we know to have dialects. Otherwise, avian dialects are known to us only from bird song. To familiarize ourselves with song dialects, we can begin again with the chaffinch.

In some regions the male chaffinch appends a short, pregnant 'kit' (Fig. 54) to his complete strophe; in other areas he does not. Figure 55 will suggest to the reader how widespread this song variation is. It sums up the present state of our knowledge, but we can say with certainty that it is incomplete. A complete chart would have

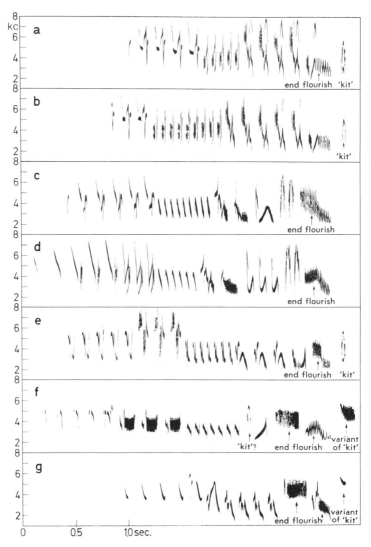

Fig. 54. (a-g) Chaffinch strophes. (a) and (d) from the same male; (b) and (c) from the same male. (a), (b), (e) with concluding 'kit'. (f) and (g) with variants of 'kit' for their close. (a) and (b), (c) and (d) respectively, are strophes of the same type. Places recorded: (a, b, c, d) southwestern Germany; (e) Graz (Austria); (f, g) the Dolomites (northern Italy). The same end flourish (c, d, e) appears in widely separated locations.

to contain many more dots, do densely packed together in places that we would end up with a big black smear on the paper.

The 'kit' of the chaffinch is of interest, first and foremost, because it is so similar to the alarm 'kit' of our three woodpecker species (*Dendrocopus;* see Fig. 55). Now we can conceive three possible ways in which this similarity came about: (1) the woodpeckers learned it from the chaffinches; (2) the chaffinches eavesdropped on the woodpeckers and picked it up from them; (3) each developed it independently of the other. The first possibility is ruled out right away, because no woodpecker is in a position to imitate vocal sounds. The third possibility cannot be refuted, but the second possibility seems more likely to me. We do find great similarities between the vocalizations of different species, even in cases where there is no question of reciprocal learning or a common origin. The alarm calls of our fieldfare and the Indian green-backed tit are cases in point. But in spite of their similarity, these calls do differ in fine details. And that difference in detail is precisely what we do not find in the 'kit' of the chaffinch and the woodpecker. Only the loudness of the woodpecker's 'kit' is not matched by the chaffinch's 'kit'; hence the latter sound lacks overtones above 6 kilocycles. On the whole the chaffinch limits itself to imitating members of its own species, but now and then it will also pick up something from another species.

The 'kit' of the chaffinch is not the only instance where something alien to a species is used as a dialect. In many districts one treecreeper species (*Certhia familiaris*) will append a call of its sibling species to its own strophe, while in other districts it is not present.

At first I believed that the 'kit' was the one and only variant at the end of an otherwise complete chaffinch strophe. Then colleagues called my attention to different elements which show up in the Dolomites (Fig. 54). So here again the mosaic-like pattern is not composed of just two blocks—'kit' present, 'kit' absent; it is composed of more variations than that.

Normally a chaffinch strophe ends with a 'flourish' (Fig. 54). The flourish has many variants, and bird lovers have fancy names for the most striking ones. In some areas one particular end flourish predominates, in other areas another flourish does; and the same final song element can show up in widely separated areas (Fig. 54). No one has investigated this matter thoroughly yet. Indeed it is a difficult question, since almost all chaffinches are in command of several strophes which may vary greatly. The situation here is quite akin to that we saw in the case of the yellowhammer and the marsh tit (chapter 5, p. 37). Like them, the chaffinch sings one type of strophe for awhile and then switches to another; hence you must wait a long time to tape the complete repertoire of a chaffinch. The patience required to do this, together with the work required to make sound spectrograms of the songs, has not been invested so far. It is a pity because we are in fact very well informed about the innate and learned portions of chaffinch song.

Little more is known about the chaffinch's strophe dialects than about its end flourish. Nevertheless Conrads (1966) was able to show that in many areas almost all the males have closely corresponding strophes in their repertoire, e.g., figure 54 a and b, c and d, respectively. With respect to the four chaffinch dialects described above, we do not know precisely how many male chaffinches deviate from the prevailing type in any case. In some areas several dialects show up in about equal proportions; thus we find three prevailing strophes sung by 24 percent, 28 percent, and 35 percent of the males respectively.

Short-toed treecreepers lend themselves more readily to this sort of study because most males have only one strophe of a very stereotyped sort. A few males do alternate between two strophe types, but both are quite stereotyped

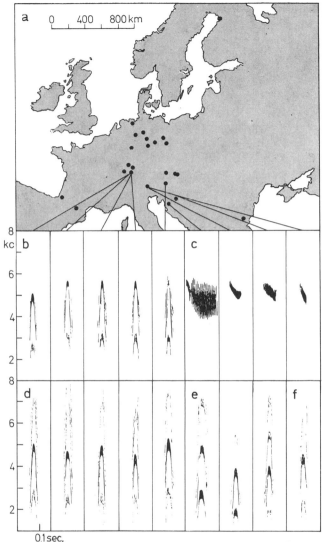

FIG. 55. (a) Chart with places where chaffinches append a wood-pecker-like 'kit' to their strophe, (b) 'kit' of five male chaffinches, (c) 'kit' variants of four male chaffinches. The lines are connected with the places where they were recorded. (d) 'kit' of *Dendrocopus major*, (e) 'kit' of *Dendrocopus medius*, (f) 'kit' of *Dendrocopus minor*.

(Fig. 56). A further advantage of the treecreeper's strophe is its brevity.

The stereotypy is so extensive that almost all the strophe elements of different males can be compared with one another; this is particularly true of the last three elements in the strophe (Fig. 57). In some areas the songs of different males are so similar that one would be inclined to attribute all the strophes to one male (Fig. 57 a–i). In other regions the differences between them are greater (Fig. 57 k–s). One of the factors indicating great stereotypy or clear variation within a given population is the number of elements per strophe. Seven of the nine males in Ludwigsburg have six elements in their strophe (Fig. 57 a–g). Only two diverge from this pattern, having five elements in their strophe (Fig. 57 h and i). One of the Frankfurt treecreepers has two strophe types with a different number of elements. One type contains seven elements, the other contains six (Fig. 57 k and l). In four cases the strophes of the remaining males have six elements; in three cases they have five elements (Fig. 57 m–s).

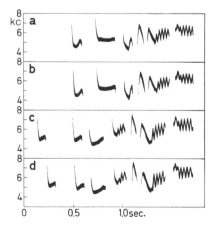

Fig. 56 *a–d*. Four strophes of a short-toed treecreeper. (*a, b*) Same strophe type, (*c, d*) same strophe type.

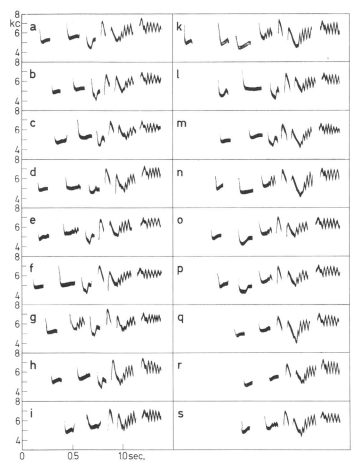

FIG. 57 *a–s*. Short-toed treecreeper strophes from 17 males: (*a–i*) from Ludwigsburg; (*k–s*) from Frankfurt. Strophes (*k*) and (*l*) come from the same male.

If we use different symbols to chart places with great or little variation within a population, we again end up with a mosaic pattern such as the one we saw in the case of chaffinch dialects (Fig. 53).

We get the same result with elements (e) and (E) of the treecreeper strophe (Fig. 58), ending up with twelve different types. They are highly uniform within a given area: shared by 18 of 23 males in Oldenburg, 17 of 19 males in Ludwigsburg, and 23 of 25 males in La Granja (central Spain). The same type (3) shows up both in southern Germany and in the Spanish Pyrenees; between these two areas are other dialects. In one case the boundary line between two dialects runs through a small wood which lies between two forest ranges. Of the four males in this little wood, two sing one type, one sings the other type, and one sings a mixture of both.

Having established that two features of treecreeper song show mosaic-like variation, we now would like to find out whether they are linked with each other. To do this, we take a look at figure 57. In both populations the penultimate element is of the same type. Thus we have the same dialect in two regions which differ in another feature—in differing degrees among different males in fact. We saw above that this feature likewise shows mosaic-like variations. If we chart both mosaic patterns on transparent paper separately and then overlay them, they will not coincide. Therefore the dialects of different parts of the same song are independent of one another.

In four regions I have kept tabs on treecreeper dialects over a period of six to nine years. In all that time the formation of elements (e) and (E) has not changed. As a matter of fact, one remarkable strophe dialect of the chaffinch dominated a region for a period of at least twenty years (Conrads, 1966).

Small birds, such as treecreepers and chaffinches, have a slim life expectancy. An individual bird can live for many years, to be sure, but after one year newborn birds replace at least a third of all the individuals. Thus dialects must be passed on to the younger generation, for otherwise it would not be possible for so many males in a region to have concordant songs and calls. We may as-

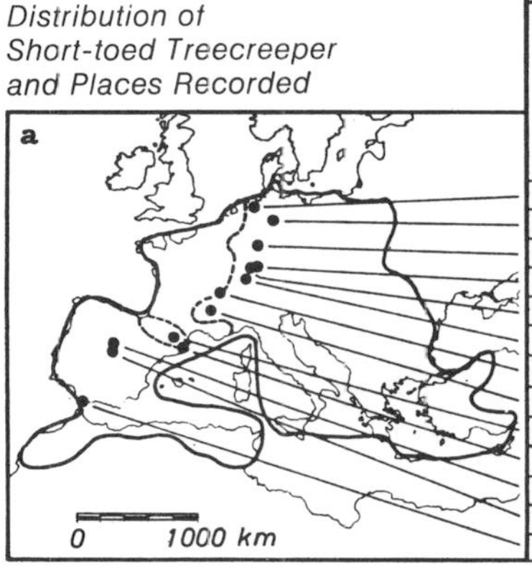

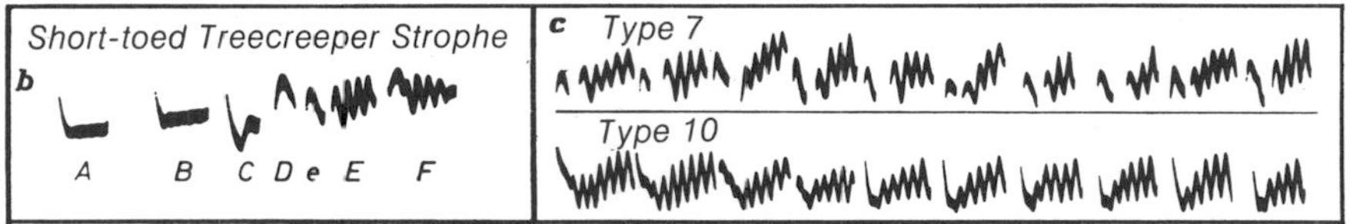

d Types of Elements e and E

Place Recorded	n	1	2	3	4	5	6	7	8	9	10	11	12
Oldenburg	23	3	18					2					
Braunschweig	6		1	3			2						
Gießen	3						1	2					
Ludwigsburg	19			17		2					(1)		
Rastatt	7			6		1(1)							
Freiburg	26		4					22					
Lyon	5							5					
Valence	10			2	5								3
Puigcerda	3			3									
Gerona	8			1					7				
La Granja	25			(1)						1	23(1)	1	
San Rafael	5									5			
Jimena	13			1					1			4	7

FIG. 58. (*a*) Distribution of the short-toed treecreeper and places recorded. (*b*) Strophe of the short-toed treecreeper. (*c*) Type 7 and type 10 of elements *e* and *E* from different males. (*d*) Places recorded, number of males recorded (*n*), and the frequency of twelve types of elements *e* and *E*. The dotted lines in (*a*) indicate the western limits of the treecreeper's distribution.

sume that bird dialects can remain constant over a much longer period than we have actually known so far. It is simply that we have not yet devoted enough time to the matter to be able to prove it.

If we collate the results of dialect research, we come up with the following picture. Dialects are found in both avian song and avian calls. A whole strophe or parts of it may go to make up the dialect. When it is composed of parts of the strophe, they come toward the end of the strophe. But dialects can also arise insofar as all the males of one locality agree completely, while those of another locality differ individually in their songs. If several dialects appear in the song of one species, they are independent of one another. Some or almost all the males in a relatively broad area have uniform calls or song. A different version can predominate in the next adjoining area. The boundary between the two dialects can be hard and fast; or it can be composed of an intermediate zone where males sing both variations or a mixture of both. The same dialect can show up in widely separated areas, with different versions prevailing in the areas between them. If we use different colors to chart the different dialects on a map, we end up with a multi-colored mosaic; and the sections with the same color may be far apart (Fig. 53). In a given region dialects remain constant for years, and they are handed down to newborn birds. We shall now try to describe how the latter process takes place.

Thanks to banding, we know that most young of many species settle down near their birthplace. No particular direction is preferred when living conditions are equally favorable on all sides. Suppose a male chaffinch or a male treecreeper is born at point o (Fig. 53). It is a matter of chance whether he will settle in dialect area a, b, or c the following year. Three brother birds may settle in three different dialect areas. If they are chaffinches, then each one will use a different rain call, a different end flourish, or a different strophe to proclaim his territory to rivals or to attract a mate. They could not have inherited these features from their father, so the only possible alternative is learning. This is not just a conclusion we are compelled to draw from our premises; it is something for which we have concrete proof.

White-crowned sparrows of North America have clear-cut dialects which are particularly noticeable in the trill

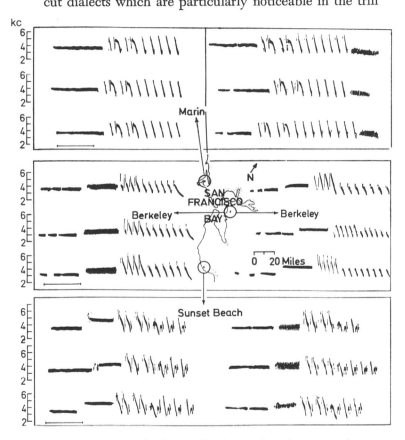

FIG. 59. One strophe from each of 18 males white-crowned sparrows. Within a given sector the variation is small. It is greater from one sector to the next, particularly in the second half of the strophe. The time lines on the horizontal axis represent 0.5 seconds. (After Marler and Tamura, 1964.)

portion of their song (Fig. 59). Marler and Tamura (1964) took young white-crowned sparrows from the nest and raised them. So great was the acoustic isolation that they were not able to hear any adult bird of their species. None of them produced the dialect of the area from which they had come (Fig. 60); all of them in the group sang uniformly. To be sure, the conformity was not as close as between neighboring birds in the wild. But the differences in song between birds in solitary isolation is fundamentally greater.

The experiment turned out differently when self-reliant young birds, 30 to 100 days old, were captured and then

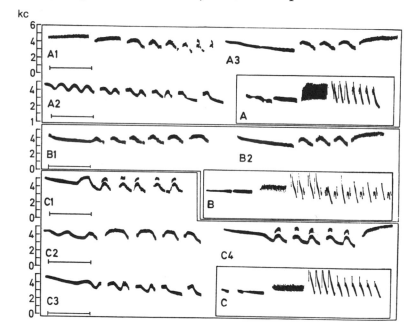

Fig. 60.   One strophe from each of nine male white-crowned sparrows from three dialect areas (*A, B, C*). From the age of three to nine days, the nine males were kept as a group in acoustic isolation. *A1* to *A3* are the strophes of three hand-raised males from dialect area *A;* the same setup applies to *B* and *C*. The time line is 0.5 seconds long. (After Marler and Tamura, 1964.)

raised in acoustic isolation. The next spring they developed a strophe which showed no differences from those of adult males in the place of capture (Fig. 61). Thus in order to develop their own strophe later in accordance with the dialect of the area, all these birds needed was to hear the song of wild males of the species shortly after leaving the nest. At this age the juveniles no longer allowed themselves to be influenced by the strophe of another dialect area when it was played to them. Thus juveniles between 30 and 100 days old must already be in the area where they will breed the following year; otherwise there would be more males who deviated from the prevailing dialect. From Lührl's investigations of the collared flycatcher (1959) we know that a long migration can intervene between the time of imprinting in their future home region and their actual settlement there the next spring. But the flycatchers do return to the place of imprinting.

With chaffinches the situation is somewhat different from that of the white-crowned sparrow. Their song, too, is open to influence in the first months of their life. But they learn the fine details of dialect only in the spring of their second year—at their breeding grounds.

A percentage of the males in a given region deviate from the prevailing dialect. Among short-toed treecreep-

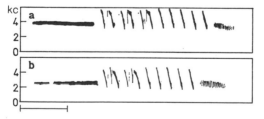

Fig. 61. (*a*) Strophe of a male captured at about the age of 30 to 100 days and kept in acoustic isolation from then on; his strophe shows a remarkable correspondence with the dialect of the place of capture (*b*). The time line is 0.5 seconds. (After Marler and Tamura, 1964.)

ers it is 15 percent for elements (e) and (E). We do not know the background history of these males who deviate from the 'correct' dialect. Perhaps they were resettled as adult birds, after their song had already become fixed.

It is not only the male white-crowned sparrow that is imprinted with the wild song of adult members of the species; young females are too, as a simple experiment proved. Normally most female birds do not sing. But as we shall see in more detail later, many birds can be induced to sing by the male sex hormone (testosterone). It works with males and females. When female white-crowned sparrows were so treated, they sang the song of the species perfectly—in the dialect of their place of capture.

In short, dialects appear to play an important role in avian social life. But we do not know what this role is.

As we have already seen, dialects are maintained through tradition. The agents in the process are probably not the father birds as such but rather males in the area. Only for a brief period are young birds receptive to the fine details of song, and this period coincides with their first stay in their future breeding grounds.

The historical origin of dialects is obscure. One characteristic of another bird may offer us a clue as to how they could have arisen. We know that whinchats imitate one avian species for awhile, and then another species—the imitations always depending on the sound repertoire of the surrounding area. All the whinchats of an area interject one particular species into their repertoire for a few days and then focus on another species. Blackbirds keep particularly striking whistles in their repertoire for a long time, but they disappear after a few years. What we are dealing with here are fashionable crazes, quite akin to those we find among human beings. Just as the hula hoop can be the craze one day and forgotten the next, so it is with avian crazes. For a brief period all will follow one vogue, then switch to another.

Now dialects may be 'petrified' fashions or various stages of them. However they may arise, dialects evince a capacity for differentiation which of itself could not lead to the split-up of a species. To go that far, other differences would have to enter the picture.

Insofar as the formation of species is concerned, however, learning capacity may well be of great importance. For learning can bring about a change quicker than heredity can—particularly when the whole population adopts what has been learned. Indeed it is quite possible that a connection exists between the acoustic learning capacity of the oscines and the profusion of their species. About one half of all birds belong to this group. And outside of this group, as far as we know, only Psittacidae and Trochilidae (and perhaps a few Strigidae) can imitate what they have heard.

In any case we are still left with the question of how a new dialect can come to prevail in a given population, since the process of assimilating and conforming to the sounds of adult birds presents a major obstacle. Now we know from long-term studies that the density of individual species fluctuates considerably. Many species, which have heavy losses in our lands during severe winters, sometimes drop down to a few individuals over a broad area. If there are alien songsters among the survivors, as there are in every population, this could give rise to new dialects. Other catastrophes besides severe winters will occur to other species over long periods of time. In terms of the present state of our knowledge, we cannot avoid assuming a drastic drop in population density to explain the origin of a dialect.

In chapter 6 we explained the great importance of song in the life of many avian species. As the behavioral scientist puts it: song is a signal. Now effective signals have to be plain and unequivocal. If they can be misunderstood, the consequences will be serious. Picture a driver, who cannot distinguish red and green colors, sitting in his car before a stoplight at a busy urban intersection. Well, a bird song that is not true to the species will have a similar effect on the propagation of the singer. He will not crash into other birds as our color-blind driver might, of course, but his chances of attracting a female of the species are slim. Admittedly there is as yet no experimental proof of this, but many signs point in this direction.

Now the transformation of a signal through learning contains a hidden danger. It may lead to fancy excrescences which will weaken the basic signal. The fact is that the songs of many species seem to contain more than they need to make the best possible appeal to members of the species. This seems very likely on the basis of Bremond's study of the robin (1968). Species with complicated songs, such as the redstart and the blackbird, must have a solid capacity for abstraction in order to ignore the superfluous sound elements. Birds with dialects may use a different tack to achieve the same goal, i.e., maintaining the efficacy of the signal.

Figure 62 illustrates one such possibility. The left side of the chart depicts a rare collection of strophes belonging to short-toed treecreepers. They come from northern Germany, southern Germany, Yugoslavia, and Spain; and they reflect the whole spectrum of this avian species. Now a female of the species in quest of a mate might not find it so easy to interpret all the strophes correctly. She might not readily interpret all of them as signals from a male short-toed treecreeper. It would be much easier for her if all males of her species were to sing as the six males on the right side of figure 62 do. But that in fact is precisely what they do for a female who is searching for a mate, because the 'horizon' of a bird is usually much more of a neighborhood affair than we would like to think.

A bird can fly thousands of miles, but even migratory birds usually settle down in the vicinity of their birthplace. There a female short-toed treecreeper will encounter males in two or three dialect areas at most. Usu-

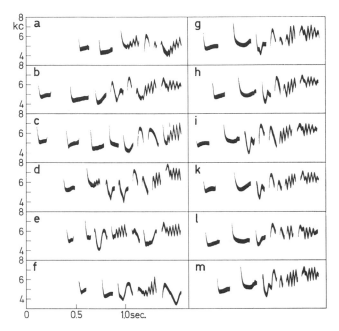

FIG. 62 *a–m*. One strophe from each of twelve male short-toed treecreepers: (*a*) northern Germany, (*b*) southern Germany, (*c*) central Spain, (*d*) Yugoslavia, (*e, f*) central Spain, (*g–m*) Freiburg (southern Germany).

ally she will achieve her goal in the first area. So the signals that are important for a female will not vary as the strophes on the left side of figure 62 do. Frequently they will show little more variation than the six strophes on the right side of the chart do. And it is certainly easier to recognize all six on the right as treecreeper songs than it is to recognize all six on the left as such. Thus dialects improve the effectiveness of song as a signal by setting limits on its variability. That is one explanation of why birds have dialects. But is it correct?

X. The Evolution of New Species

a) What are species?

In the preceding chapters we have repeatedly spoken about animal species. But what is a species? The answer seems simple enough. An animal species is a group of individuals who, under natural circumstances, propagate with each other unrestrictedly. In these terms higher animals readily lend themselves to classification into species when they inhabit the same region. But the area of animal species is usually not unbroken and devoid of gaps, hence it is not so easy to decide whether they would cross unrestrictedly with each other under natural circumstances. The emphasis here is on 'natural circumstances' because in captivity different species will often cross without much trouble.

If two groups of individuals are not present in the same region, we must analyze how different they are and then compare the findings with similar species that live in the selfsame region without intermixing. In this way we can determine whether geographically separated individuals belong to one species or two. This determination is not absolutely certain of course. Therefore, we cannot say that there are 8611 bird species in the world. We can only say that there are approximately 8600 bird species. That does not bother us here, for we are more interested in the fascinating question: How do new animal species arise?

b) Barriers to procreation

Like Dobzhansky we shall use the term 'isolation mechanisms' to refer to the factors which prevent a crossing between two groups of individuals. These factors can crop up at very different points. If two groups of individuals breed in the same region, but at different times of year or in different milieus, then they will not get together with each other. Even if they do meet, behavioral barriers can prevent pair formation. The movements and vocal sounds of one group may be incomprehensible to the other group. Such factors, or even their odor alone in the case of many animals, has an isolating effect. A potential partner from a different group may even be ignored because of its unusual coloring. A yellow ring around the eye instead of a red ring may sometimes suffice to prevent mating, as Smith's studies of gulls (1966) have shown. The factor listed under (1 c) below plays only a subordinate role, if any at all, in the case of birds.

The three isolation mechanisms just mentioned prevent hybridization *before* fertilization of the egg. After fertilization other factors have an inhibiting effect. The following classification of isolation mechanisms is based on Mayr (1967):

1. Mechanisms which prevent species hybridization
   a) Potential mates do not meet each other
      (seasonal and environmental isolation)
   b) Potential mates meet but do not pair
      (behavioral isolation)
   c) Copulation is attempted, but sperm does not pass over
      (mechanical isolation)

2. Mechanisms which prevent the complete success of species hybridization
   a) Sperm is transmitted, but the egg is not fertilized
      (genetic mortality)
   b) The egg is fertilized but dies
      (zygote mortality)
   c) Hybrids are generated, but their viability is reduced
      (Hybrid incapacity for life)
   d) The hybrids are fully viable, but they are sterile or produce defective offspring
      (hybrid sterility)

The female body can react defensively against the spermatozoid of another species, thus preventing the fertilization or later development of the egg. The germ plasm of male and female cannot be too different if it is to produce viable offspring; for in the growth of a higher living organism from the union of egg and spermatozoid to a fully developed animal there are many processes which work in synchronization. Excessively great differences lead to the sterility or the diminished viability of the hybrid.

As we have just noted, two animal species must not produce completely sterile offspring—or no offspring at all. In the case of the higher animals at least, mechanisms seem to develop which prevent pairing in the first place. Among birds the primary mechanisms of this sort are forms of movement, vocalizations, and color patterns. In most cases, however, more than one factor combines to ensure the separation of different species.

c) *The first steps*

No two animals which result from the fusion of spermatozoid and egg are identical. Each differs from others in many details of its germ plasm, which come to be through mutations and new combinations of genes. Some portion of the mutations are deleterious and their bearers are quickly wiped out.

The areas of most avian species stretch over wide regions with very different environmental factors. Depending on the nature of these conditioning factors, dark coloration is more suitable in one region and light coloration in another. Since those of deleterious coloration or size have slimmer chances of survival and hence fewer offspring, those most suited for a given environment prove to be successful and prevail.

The house sparrow is a good example of this. In 1859 house sparrows were set free in North America. They had not existed here before. In a short time they settled down over enormous expanses of territory. Many populations have not had even fifty years to differentiate themselves; yet already their coloration has adapted to their environment so that it matches other avian species indigeneous to a given region.

The individual groups of an avian species can indeed intermix. But within a greater area they do differ both in their germ plasm and in external features. Deviation from other groups is especially accelerated among those groups whose range of distribution is broken up by barriers. This is particularly true when the uninhabitable areas in between are broad enough to prevent or severely limit interchange of individuals.

In this connection we shall take another look at the song of the short-toed treecreeper—specifically at element (F). From figure 63 we may infer that there is an extraordinary conformity with respect to type 1 over a wide area; this conformity ranges from northern Germany to northern Spain. In three areas of central and southern Spain, by contrast, there is a different type, or the element is absent. Within the isolated regions, however, element F is produced very uniformly in the south as well.

How do we explain this distribution pattern? For its living milieu the short-toed treecreeper needs coarse-barked old trees in about the same density we find in public gardens, orchards and forests. These preconditions are met in the area running from northern Germany to northeast Spain; there are no great gaps there. In central and southern Spain, by contrast, we find broad areas that are woodless or, at the very least, devoid of old trees. Between the islands of forest in Spain, the landscape offers no living place to a short-toed treecreeper. In the sparse woodlands of Spain the treecreeper lives like a land bird stranded on an island and surrounded by the sea. Under such conditions interchange between populations is severely hindered. This obstacle is not present in the unbroken area to the north.

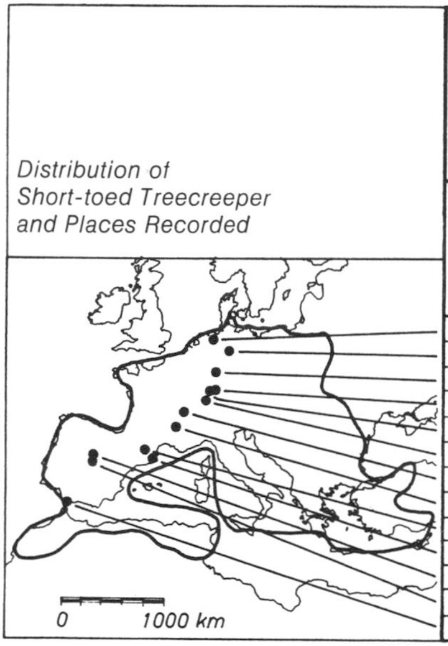

		Short-toed Treecreeper Strophe			
		A B C D e E F			

		Types of Element F			
		1	2	3	4
Place Recorded	n				Absent
Oldenburg	23	23			
Braunschweig	6	6			
Gießen	2	2			
Ludwigsburg	19	19			
Rastatt	7	7			
Freiburg	26	26			
Lyon	5	5			
Valence	10	9			1
Puigcerda	3	3			
Gerona	8	6			2
La Granja	25	1		23	1(1)
San Rafael	5				5
Jimena	14		14		

Distribution of Short-toed Treecreeper and Places Recorded

0   1000 km

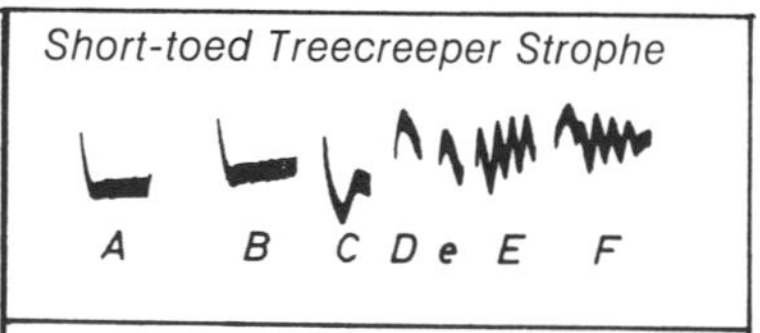

FIG. 63. Geographical variation in the last element (F) of the short-toed treecreeper's strophe. The last element is completely uniform from northern Germany to northern Spain. In central and southern Spain, by contrast, each population has a different version.

Not only are the Spanish populations isolated; the number of individuals in them is also smaller. To what extent this accelerates a course of development which deviates from the main area is uncertain. In all likelihood the stock would have to drop to a few individuals before it could truly effect a rapid differentiation. We can be quite certain that more than once in the past 5000 years the stock has been radically decimated by catastrophes, e.g., long persistent drought, wetness, or cold. In a small area such conditions 'impoverish' the germ plasm (as well as the range of variation acquired through learning) much more than they do in a large area—if we assume the same rate of reduction.

In model laboratory experiments on the fruit fly, Dobzhansky and his co-workers followed the development of ten small and then large populations. The large populations started with 4000 individuals in each case; the small populations started with 20 individuals (Fig. 64). Four

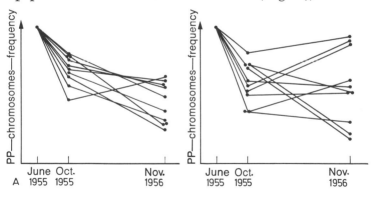

FIG. 64. Twenty fruit fly populations which came from the same parent population but were raised in isolation from one another. The populations on the left side were started with 4000 individuals each; those on the right with 20 individuals each. After 17 months, i.e., many generations later, the variation between the populations on the right was greater than that between the populations on the left. The vertical scale indicates the percentage of specific chromosomes. (After Dobzhansky and Pavlovsky in Mayr, 1967.)

months later the fraction of specific mutations[1] in the individual populations varied. In the large populations the range of population deviation remained the same after an additional thirteen months, whereas it jumped noticeably in the other group (Fig. 64). Yet all twenty populations were descendants of the same parent populations. So the experiment indicates two things: (1) the effect of isolation, because no interchange was possible between the twenty populations and (2) the end result of a reduction to a few individuals.

Now we can see directly the effect of isolation in the short-toed treecreepers of Spain. But we cannot say for sure whether these populations were in fact reduced to a few individuals at some point.

The last ice age, which ended about 10,000 years ago, made northern and central Eurasia uninhabitable for many avian species. Ice and frost destroyed the woodlands. We know this from several sources, one of them being the so-called pollen diagrams. Each year a layer of pollen is deposited in the marshes of Eurasia—along with other fine-grained material. Pollen is contained in the male spores of anemophylous plants, which are scattered by the wind in every direction. The dense array of these pollen-laden spores causes much distress to victims of hay fever. This pollen is of great importance to science, because under the microscope the fossil pollen grains reveal their nature to the expert. Thus we get information about which plants were growing in Eurasia during an earlier period.

The composite picture constructed from many studies leads us to a clear and unmistakeable conclusion: during the last ice age woodlands disappeared in our region and in many other parts of the world. Forest-dwelling animals

---

1. Mutations are alterations in the genetic carrier which are passed on to descendants and thus serve as the basis for the gradual alteration of living organisms in the course of geological history.

had to retreat to the regions shaded black in Figure 65. This splintered the area of many species which had previously been widespread in the north. Isolation was now able to operate as a factor. The nature and degree of separate development was very different among the individual forms. This is not just theory, as the following examples will show.

In northern and eastern Europe long-tailed tits are white-crowned; in western and southern Europe they are striped. In central Europe we find both forms and a whole range of transitional forms in between (Fig. 66); they cross with each other unrestrictedly and are productive. From the distribution chart we can infer that the white-crowned tits spent the ice age in far easterly sanctuaries of southern Asia, while the stripe-crowned tits spent the ice age in southerly sanctuaries (Stresemann, 1919). After the ice age was over, the white-crowned tits and the stripe-crowned tits headed back as far as central Europe. Since the difference between them is limited to a head marking, and since this apparently plays no role in mutual recognition, the two forms intermix. If they did not have such strikingly different coloration, we would know nothing about the probable history of their distribution.

Fig. 65. Refuge areas for woodland animals during the last ice age. (After Reinig, 1938, altered.)

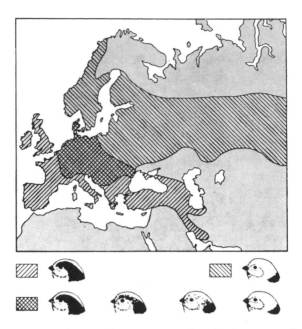

Fig. 66. Distribution of stripe-crowned and white-crowned long tailed tits, and the mixed area in which both 'pure' forms and the whole range of intermediate forms are present. (Lower portion of the illustration is after Niethammer, but altered.)

In the song of the short-toed treecreeper and the color distribution of the long-tailed tit we can see the first steps toward a split-up which may one day lead to new species. But the chances of reaching this stage are slim because the isolation is often broken too early, as we learn from the long-tailed tits.

d) A few steps further

Carrion crow and hooded crow.—The carrion crow and the hooded crow look so different in their coloration (Fig. 67) that an unbiased observer could take them for two species. In fact they do cross with each other. The distribution pattern of the two forms, however, looks differ-

FIG. 67. Carrion crow and hooded crow.

ent from that of the long-tailed tit. In this case there is no broad area of intermingling; there is only a slender zone (Fig. 68) which is very constant. It was charted for the first time in 1887, and the second study followed in 1928. No essential change from 1887 was to be noted, and this

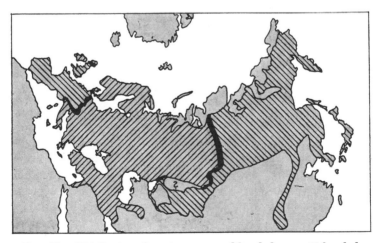

FIG. 68. Distribution of carrion crow and hooded crow: ▨ hooded crow, ■ hybrid zone, ▧ carrion crow. (After Meise, 1928, altered.)

holds true up to the present. We do not know why the carrion and hooded crows do not extend their areas onto one another. It would be clear if the explanation were that there are restrictions on intermingling or that the hybrids are disadvantaged in some way. Obviously the differentiation did not go so far as to lead to the formation of a new species. What is worth noting is the presence of the purely black form in both the western and eastern sectors of the area. On the basis of that datum, the hooded crow must have originated in a refuge area where it changed sharply. Meanwhile the form present in the east and west underwent little change, to all appearances at least.

Chiffchaff.—In chapter 5 we became acquainted with the chiffchaff, whose song varies only slightly from the Arctic Circle to southern France. In Spain, Portugal, North Africa and the Canary Islands, however, the chiffchaffs sing something completely different (Figs. 69 and 70). In terms of song one could take the two forms to be two species, but this interpretation is refuted by the presence of a mixed zone in southwest France amid the spurs of the Pyrenees. In this zone some males handle both song forms while others display a whole range of intermediate stages.

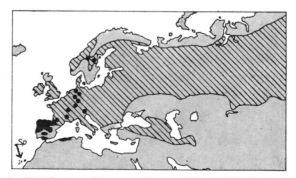

FIG. 69. Distribution of two song forms of the chiffchaff: ■ Spanish song form • places where 'normal' songs were recorded, ▨ remaining distribution of the chiffchaff.

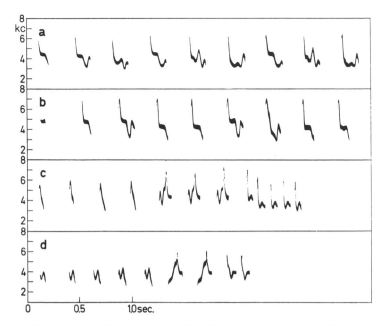

FIG. 70. (*a*) Strophe of a chiffchaff in northern Sweden, (*b*) strophe of a chiffchaff in southwestern Germany, (*c, d*) strophes of two Spanish chiffchaffs.

At one point the borderline is quite sharply drawn. On one side of the French town of Pau the chiffchaffs sing like the other northern chiffchaffs; on the other side they sing like the chiffchaffs in Spain. On the Atlantic coast the transitional zone is wider.

The chiffchaffs of Siberia sing something completely different again (Fig. 71). We do not know how uniform their song is or how large their song area is. Up to now we have only one recording of one bird, and the only other source of information is a few descriptions by travelling researchers which offer little in the way of explanation.

The distribution pattern of the chiffchaff's song forms is very similar to that of the carrion and hooded crow. Like the mosaic pattern of dialects they are quite uniform in one region and the boundary lines are relatively sharp. In contrast to the dialects, however, the qualitative differences in the song forms are so great that we would ordinarily expect to find them between different species.

This marked intraspecific difference apparently developed during a period of isolation. In other words, the populations which are so markedly different today must have been geographically separated at some earlier time. The cause of their spatial isolation could have been some sort of climatic catastrophe once again, e.g., the ice age, which has left such a profound mark on today's animal world.

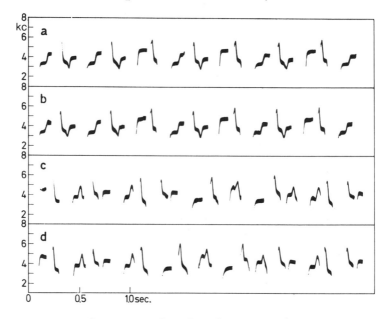

FIG. 71 *a–d*. Four strophes of a Siberian chiffchaff. (After a recording by Veprinstev and Naoomova, 1964.)

The external features of the crow and the song forms of the chiffchaff diverged in some period of isolation. But they did not diverge so much that each side acted like an independent species when they met later on. The separation did not last long enough, so the species split only went part of the way.

Great tit.—Clearly the great tit is one step closer to the 'split-up' into different species. Its area extends in a wide belt from England to Japan. The southern portion of the distribution ring runs through southern Asia into the Mediterranean region (Fig. 72). On a chart it does look like a ring in any case.

In the north the area is pretty continuous and unbroken, but that is not the case in the south. There steppes, deserts, and mountains make up large sections which are bypassed even by small birds migrating between their breeding region and their winter quarters. The extent of these barriers severely limits the interchange of brooding birds between the individual populations. The result is a splintering into 36 races[2] within the southern portion of the distribution ring. From England to the Pacific, on the other hand, there are only three.

The races can be divided into three or four large groups. Great tits of the *major* group look like our European great tits, with their yellow belly and their green back. Great tits of the *minor* group have a white belly and a green back. The *cinereus* great tits are light gray on their belly and back. The fourth group, *bokharensis,* is one on which scholars are divided. They cannot agree whether this group is already a separate species of its own or not. *Bokharensis* is an inhabitant of Turkestan, where ornithologists are not to be found in such thick clusters; hence our knowledge of them is quite meager. The only thing that is certain is that *bokharensis* is closely related to the great tit, as are two other species in India, i.e., the green-backed tit and the black-spotted yellow tit.

---

2. Races are groups of populations which differ from each other in color or size. Ordinarily no isolation mechanisms are operative between them.

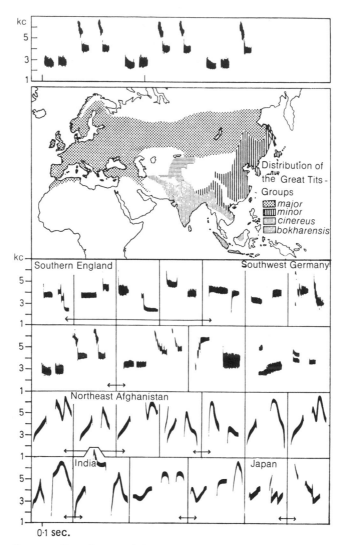

FIG. 72. Distribution of the four large groups of great tits. Underneath are song portions of the great tit, which are arranged in strophes (top). Element groups from different strophes of the same male are indicated with two-headed arrows. The elements of European and south or east Asian great tits show fundamental differences. (After Gompertz, 1968.)

As we said, the split-up among the great tits is greatest in the southern section of their area. These differences are not limited to outward appearances. Every European is probably familiar with the song of our domestic great tit —its charming 'zizibebe'. The repetition of a group of elements characterizes almost all its strophes (Fig. 73). If we compare the strophe components of English and German great tits we can readily see their basic agreement in principle—both in their strophe structure and in the form of the elements (Fig. 72).

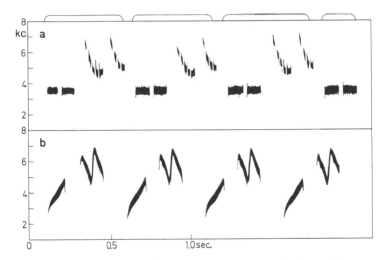

FIG. 73. (*a*) Strophe of a European great tit. Each strophe arranges a group of elements; in this strophe there are four. (*b*) Strophe of an Afghan great tit. Like the European strophe, it repeats a group of elements. But the quality of the elements and their timbre is essentially different in (*a*) and (*b*).

If one were listening to the song of a great tit in India or Afghanistan and did not see the bird, one would be more inclined to think that he was listening to a coal tit. The strophe structure and the repetition is like that of the European bird, but the form and the timbre of the elements is fundamentally different. A quick comparison of the songs in figure 72 will reveal this, and our European great tits behave correspondingly when a strophe of the Afghan bird is played to them (Fig. 74). Usually they do not react at all; or else they react as they would to the song of other tit species. Only a larger store of material will tell us to what extent small differences in song exist between the Afghan, Indian, and Japanese great tits.

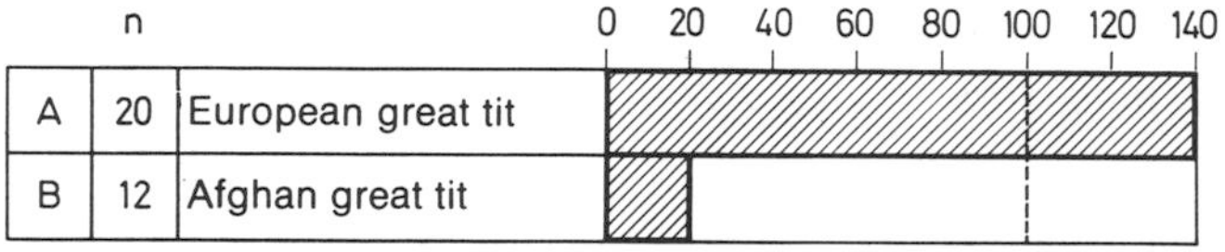

Fig. 74. (*A*) The strophe from figure 73 *a* was played ten times to European great tits; then, after a pause of two minutes, it was played to them ten more times. The number of males who were attracted by the second series is equal to 100 (dash line). The number of males attracted by the first strophe is in a ratio to that (columns). (*B*) Same experiment as (*A*) except that in the first series Afghan strophes (73 *b*) were played to them. (*n*) is the number of males tested.

It was a regular practice to transport great tits from India to Europe. Indian merchants used them as filler material in their shipments, but bird fanciers in Europe have not been greatly taken by them. An Englishwoman, Terry Gompertz, bought a pair and brought them into contact with English great tits—both in captivity and in the wild. The antipathy between the tits of different extraction was deep and mutual. Evidently some of their vocalizations are so different that they no longer recognize each other as members of the same species. We do not know whether movement patterns and their different appearance also play a role here. Terry Gompertz did manage to get hybrids from an English male and an Indian female, but only because the two captive birds had no other choice. The offspring of this pair looked and sang like Indian great tits, and they stayed around their birthplace for weeks after they were set free. No song duels or sexual advances took place between these hybrids and the birds native to the area.

If Indian and European great tits were to meet under natural circumstances, they apparently would behave like two different species. In some sectors of the great tit's area, differentiation has evidently progressed to a species split-up.

e) Twin species

Treecreeper *familiaris*[3] (*Certhia familiaris*) and the short-toed treecreeper (*Certhia brachydactyla*) look so alike that they were regarded as one species for a long time. Their differences did not escape the keen eyes of the elder Brehm, who in 1820 described the short-toed treecreeper as a second treecreeper species present here in Germany. Another gifted contemporary of his, Johann Friedrich Naumann, disputed the existence of two species; but in this case Brehm proved to be right. Up to the present day we have not found any hybrids between the two species, and even in captivity strong barriers stand in the way of species hybridization.

The distribution of the southwestern form (short-toed treecreeper) and the eastern form (treecreeper *familiaris*), and the region in which both are present (Fig. 75), bear a striking resemblance to the distribution pattern of the long-tailed tit which we saw earlier (Fig. 66). Indeed it was Stresemann who explained both distribution patterns in the same way back in 1919. According to him, the parent form of the two treecreeper species was split up into an eastern and a southwestern form during the last ice age. During this period of isolation their development diverged. Since then treecreeper *familiaris* prefers woods with smooth-barked trees, which in Germany means beech trees, spruces, and firs. The short-toed treecreeper

---

3. Translator's note: I use *familiaris* in this section to keep the two species clear and distinct in the discussion.

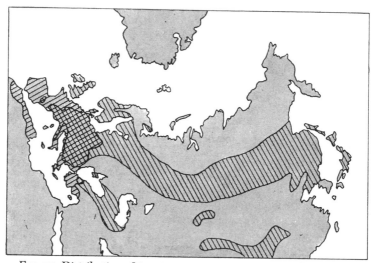

FIG. 75. Distribution of two treecreeper species: ▨ *Certhia brachy-dactyla,* ⊠ both species, ▧ *Certhia familiaris.*

will accept even gardens and sparse parks, so long as they contain coarse-barked trees. Since there is no absolute split between these two environments, we find both species in many localities.

In Scandinavia treecreeper *familiaris* is one of the few avian species which winters there despite the long Arctic night. Its good adaptation to cold is evident in our country as well. Only when the temperature drops to ($-14°C$) will treecreeper *familiaris* seek feather contact with others to withstand the night weather. By contrast, short-toed treecreepers sleep in clusters of up to 20 individuals throughout the winter (Fig. 45).

While we find these differences between the two species in their choice of trees and their sleeping patterns, they do not lead to isolation between them. And since both species build very similar nests at about the same time of year behind projecting tree bark, and are scarcely different in their courting behavior, we must look elsewhere for barriers that prevent species hybridization. The elder Brehm

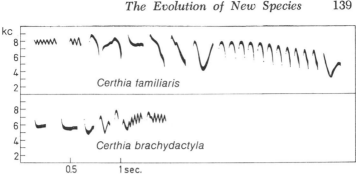

FIG. 76.   One strophe of each treecreeper species.

focused on the sound of the short-toed treecreeper as its distinguishing feature. Its song and some of its calls are fundamentally different from those of its twin species (Figs. 44, 76). In all likelihood we shall not go astray in regarding its sound as an essential barrier to species intermingling.

Sibling species do not differentiate themselves radically from other species which are also closely related; the difference is one of degree, and it is achieved gradually. In most cases they are 'recently' arisen species, and hence of particular interest for evolutionary research. We are quite certain that they acquired their differences in stages over a long period of time, as we described this process in sections (c) and (d) of this chapter.

In our European region we have a whole set of additional sibling species: chiffchaff/willow warbler; goldcrest/firecrest; pied flycatcher/collared flycatcher; nightingale/thrush nightingale; marsh tit/willow tit; arctic tern/common tern; great spotted woodpecker/syrian woodpecker. Two of them will be discussed in the following chapter.

f) The significance of species formation

As far as we know, species can arise in different ways. Over a fairly long period of time they usually do not remain the same. Changes in climate, the incursion of new species into another species area and the resultant competition for food, and many other influences make adaptations necessary. These in turn lead necessarily to changes. This course of development can be read from fossil remains. When one species has become another species through this process, we can only draw approximate conclusions by comparing the evidence with similar species who live alongside each other today.

The split up of one species into two or more species is of far greater significance for evolution (Mayr, 1967).[4] Within a procreating community single individuals or groups can alter their germ plasm from the rest only to the extent that backcrossing is still possible without a catastrophe. In other words, the interplay of hereditary factors in the partners does not allow for excessively great differences. If the genetic carriers are not in harmony, then the offspring will be less viable, sterile, or incapable of development.

The germ plasm determines the range of variation within which an animal species reacts to environmental stimuli or their absence. As biologists say, they can only occupy a given niche in any given case. At first glance it might seem that some species break through this law. The raven, for example, can inhabit high mountains and lowlands, coastal shores, and Arctic regions. As Lorenz puts it so well, unspecialization is its specialty. But there are limits imposed on the raven too. It cannot hunt at night like an owl, or dive like a tern, or even swim like a duck.

If a group of living organisms 'wants' to exhaust all the possibilities of its environment, then it must break through the hereditary fetters imposed on every species. That can only be done by splitting up into many species, i.e., by breaking up the pattern of intermixing through spatial

---

4. By 'evolution' here we mean the development of living organism in the course of geological history.

isolation. New niches are thereby opened up to the original species; and these niches will enable them to live alongside each other when they meet.[5] If there had been only one species formation in history, then there would be only one species on earth. And that species would certainly not have gotten far beyond the one-celled stage.

The first steps towards the split-up of a species will lead to a new species only in a minimum number of cases. And a minimum number of species will usher in a course of development that revolutionizes the evolutionary process. Such would be the conversion of fish into reptile, or of the latter into mammal and bird. Species are evolutionary experiments, as it were. They have a high rate of loss, but also great success—just as mutations do on another level (Mayr, 1967).

---

5. We do not know whether geographic isolation is the one and only possibility for the split-up of a species. It is a very important one in any event.

XI. *The Evolution of Sounds*

How did the common ancestor of the twin treecreeper species (*Certhia brachydactyla* and *Certhia familiaris*) sing when they were still one species? The question may seem ridiculous to some people because none of us can answer it from our own experience. There are no such things as fossilized sounds, and our ancestors of 10,000 years ago left us no descriptions. Insofar as bird sounds are concerned, we can only go back ten to thirty years into the past, i.e., as far back as recordings and tapes will permit us. Under normal circumstances that is a meaningless span of time in terms of the rise of new species.

But the situation is not as hopeless as it may seem. Comparative anatomy comes to help us in our effort to say something about the origin of living organisms. All we have to do is to examine the animals that are around us today. If one understands this technique, one can bring astonishing things to light. We discover, for example, that two of our three auditory ossicles (malleus, incus, and stapes) were once our maxillary joint. After all our ancestors were reptiles, not mammals, once upon a time; that takes us back 200–300 million years. Today these three

142

bones connect our tympanic membrane with our inner ear, intensifying sound waves picked up by the tympanic membrane and transmitting them to the inner ear. Once upon a time, however, we 'snapped up' our prey. Anatomists can prove this by comparing the bones of animals living today.[1]

The pioneer figures in behavioral research, such as Oskar Heinroth and Konrad Lorenz, were originally comparative anatomists. So it was only natural for them to use 'their' methods in investigating animal behavior. The findings did not surprise them: the more closely animals are related, the more similar their behavior patterns are. Thus behavior patterns can tell us as much about the degree of relationship between two animal species as their external appearance and bodily structure can. If we go on to investigate their albumen, their blood, their parasites, and their distribution, we will reach conclusions that should come pretty close to what is in fact their natural relationship.

Now if we are armed with this knowledge and then go on to compare such things as the song of different tit species, we cannot expect to find agreement in details. For two forms can differ completely in details, even though we may not be certain that they are in fact different species. We saw this when we compared the sounds of Afghan and European great tits (page 135). But if we examine the songs of tits[2] only in terms of their principal and basic points of agreement, the findings are positive. If we examine one common feature in twelve tit species, we find that eleven of them do have a coinciding strophe structure.

---

1. These findings are solidly supported by evidence based on extinct animals.
2. By tits here we mean only the *Parus* species of tits. We do not include other species called tits, such as the long-tailed tits and the penduline tits, which have much in common with the *Parus* species but apparently are not more intimately related with them.

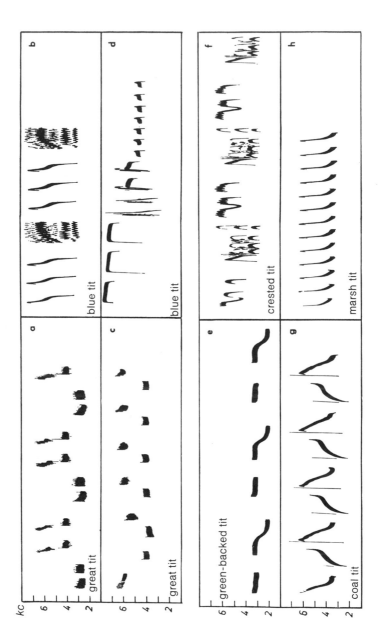

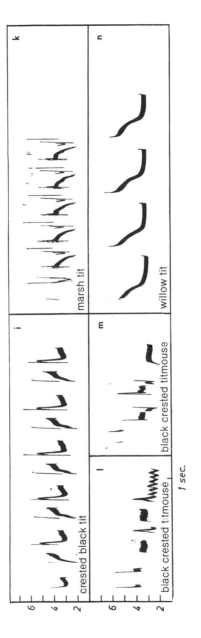

Fig. 77. Thirteen strophes of nine tit species.

As a rule tit strophes are composed of uniform elements arranged in series, as is the case with the marsh tit and the willow tit (Fig. 77 h and n); or they involve the repetition of a group of elements. Thus the great tit in figure 77 (a) sings four elements ('zizibebe') three times in succession; the fourth element is missing in the third group. The first two elements of the great tit strophe in figure 77 (c) diverge from this structural pattern, but the rest of the strophe is 'correct'. Strophes such as 77 c are rare in the case of great tits. In the case of the blue tit they are equally frequent (77 d) or even normal (77 b).

Only one of the twelve investigated species constructs its strophes in a way that differs completely from the others. It is the black crested titmouse (*Parus rubidiventris;* 77 l and m) which lives in the Himalayan woodlands and which is closely related to the European coal tit. No sound expert would attribute its song to a tit if he heard it on a recording. But it would be foolish to doubt the tit relationship of the black crested titmouse on that basis, for it closely resembles our European coal tit (*Parus ater*) and the crested black tit (*Parus melanolophus*). What is more, it builds its nest in burrows and squeezes big chunks of food with its feet to break them down into manageable bites; both of these behavior patterns are characteristic of tits and hence a good hallmark of the group.

The relationship of the black crested titmouse with two coal-tit species (*ater* and *melanolophus*) also comes from their alarm calls. Among the rest of the tit species these calls are either long drawn out or short, usually ordered sequentially, and their many 'tone bands' range over a wide pitch area (Fig. 78). Some species introduce or initiate these alarm series with completely different calls, e.g., the Indian tits (*Parus xanthogenys*) or the marsh tits and willow tits of Europe. In terms of their sound, by contrast, the three 'coal tit' species (*ater, melanolophus, rubidiventris*) have only 'introduction' calls to proclaim their

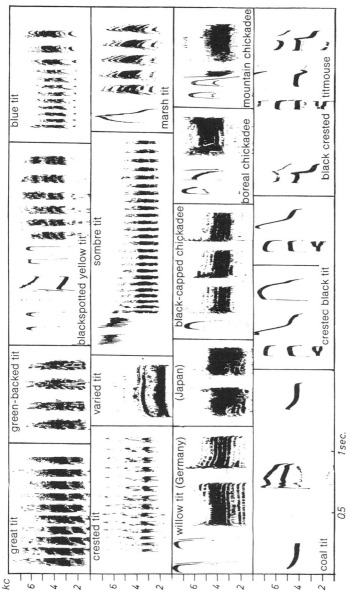

FIG. 78. Ground alarm calls of fifteen tit species.

147

alarm. They resemble each other much more than they do other tit species (Fig. 78).

One idiosyncrasy of the alarm calls of these 'coal tit' species is the polyphony of many calls. This can be seen in the second call of the coal tit (Fig. 78), where the pitch bands run in different directions and hence cannot be interpreted as a fundamental tone with overtones. We find the same feature in the first call of crested black tit (*melanophus*) and in the second call of the black crested titmouse (*rubidiventris*). In fact the latter emits six different tones simultaneously. Since this feature is not found frequently among birds, and since it is absent for the most part in other tit species, it is another support for our contention that the three 'coal tit' species are more akin to each other than to the remaining tit species.

Since our findings concur with those from other fields, we can also regard sounds as a useful indicator of kinship. Caution is in order, to be sure, as we learn from the divergent song of the black crested titmouse and the absence of common features in the dark-crowned tit species (sombre tit, marsh tit, willow tit, black-capped chickadee, boreal chickadee, and mountain chickadee). Their alarm calls are short (sombre tit), a bit longer (marsh tit), or long drawn out like the others.

The interpretation of kinship already represents a zoological application of our comparison between sounds. That brings us back to our initial question about the song and alarm calls of the common ancestors of the present-day tit species. How might they have looked on a spectrogram? Insofar as song is concerned, we can answer with some degree of certainty. The majority of tits sing according to a ground plan, which must also have been present in the song of the first tits. We cannot say that the alarm calls of the first tits probably sounded thus in an earlier day. But it seems quite certain that the common forefathers of the three 'coal tit' species did have calls more similar to these three species than to the other tit species extant today.

We would run into difficulty if we jumped right in and said that the begging call 'hip' of the one-day-old treecreeper had something to do with the sound-contact call 'srih' of the adult treecreeper. The situation is quite clear from our knowledge of the history of the 'srih' call. The development of the begging call is depicted in figure 87. In the course of the nestling stage, the simple 'hip' shifts smoothly into the sound-contact call 'srih'. Comparative anatomists discovered that juvenile development repeats phylogeny.[3] This is not always true, but it is true in 60 percent to 70 percent of the cases (Remane, 1952). To what extent behavioral patterns are recapitulated in this way remains very unclear.

To get back to our example, it is conceivable that the begging call was present earlier than the sound-contact call, in which case treecreepers have still another call with the same function. Instead of simply giving it up after it was no longer used to stimulate their parents, the treecreepers held on to it. No great change in terms of function was required because that is the same: the begging call induces parents to come right back to them; the sound-contact call induces a partner to do the same.

There is much less likelihood, however, that the begging call 'hip' earlier served as a sound-contact call and only over a period of time developed into the 'srih' call. Presumably the newly hatched treecreeper can only produce the soft and simple 'hip' call with its vocal apparatus.

Both treecreeper species (Fig. 87) transform their begging call in the same way into the sound-contact call, which varies little in the two species. Hence we may conclude that the common ancestor of both species did the same thing in a very similar way.

---

3. Phylogeny is the study of the development of a living group or form in the course of geological history.

If we compare the calls of treecreeper *familiaris* with its song, we find surprisingly solid correspondences in some respects. The sound contact 'srih', which we just noted to be the final juvenile development of the begging call, is very similar to the first song element and can be readily confused with it (Fig. 79). If we play a recording of the rivalry call, wild treecreepers (*familiaris*) will react as they do to song. They gather promptly, fly around agitatedly, and sing a great deal to expel the would-be rival. We get the same reaction if we take several treecreeper strophes, section out the element which is similar to the rivalry call, attach it to a call series, and then play it in the wild. It is very unlikely that this close correspondence between rivalry call and song element is accidental. We are pretty safe in concluding that both go back to the same source. How it all came about is a matter of conjecture so far.

On the basis of all four treecreeper forms[4] studied so far, we are readily inclined to match up individual song

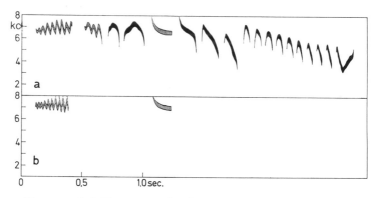

FIG. 79. (*a*) Treecreeper *familiaris* strophe. (*b*) Sound contact call 'srih' and rivalry call 'zii' of treecreeper *familiaris* which closely agree with the song elements that are shaded in the diagram.

4. We use the neutral term 'form' here instead of 'species' because we are not sure whether the American brown creeper is a separate species or simply a race of treecreeper *familiaris*.

elements with calls, as figure 80 shows. All the elements of the four strophes which correspond with calls of the respective form are shaded; the remaining elements are black. Since all four treecreeper forms evince these correspondences, that would have been the case with their common ancestors.

Worth noting is the fact that in all four forms the song elements are matched only by the sound-contact and rivalry calls, i.e., by calls whose function is also exercised by song (cf. chapter 6). That may indicate how song arose in the course of phylogenetic history. Certainly the first songbird did not sing like a nightingale. Certainly its song

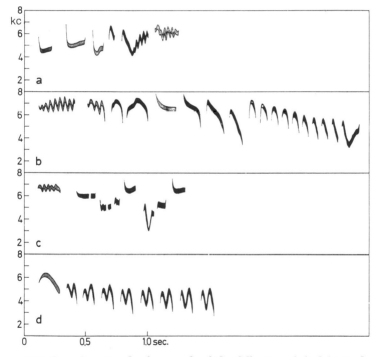

FIG. 80.   One strophe from each of the following: (*a*) short-toed treecreeper, (*b*) treecreeper *familiaris*, (*c*) brown creeper (American), (*d*) Himalayan treecreeper. The shaded elements agree closely with calls of the same species.

was simpler than bird songs are today. Sound-contact calls and rivalry calls may have been the kernel around which strophes crystallized. There are many 'maybes' here, but that in itself is a stimulus to learn more.

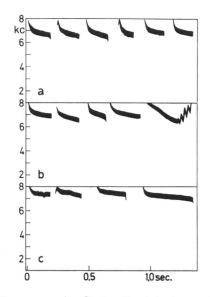

F<small>IG</small>. 81.   Treecreeper *familiaris* calls: (*a*) alarm call of six males, (*b*) rivalry calls of five males, (*c*) fright cry of four males.

If we look for further similarities in the vocalizations of treecreeper *familiaris*, the experienced expert in bird sounds can readily offer up his help. For he cannot distinguish between the treecreeper's rivalry calls and alarm calls on the basis of what he hears. Even the sound spectrogram betrays no great difference (Fig. 81). Many rivalry calls look exactly like alarm calls. Only one—on the far right in figure 81 (*b*)—deviates from the rest. Apart from that one, the only difference established so far resides not in the calls themselves but in the pauses between them. In alarm situations the pauses are quite uniform and relatively long. Confronted with a rival, treecreepers call much faster, then become quiet, then call quickly once again (Fig. 82).

The third call associated with the alarm call and the rivalry call is the fright cry, which is emitted by a treecreeper (*familiaris*) who has been seized by a male or an enemy. Some fright calls are very similar to alarm and rivalry calls; most of them, however, are drawn out (Fig. 81). In all likelihood all three calls go back to a common origin. Their similarity allows for no other assumption.

Fig. 82.   (*a*) Natural sequence of alarm calls, (*b*) of rivalry calls, (*c*) of fright cries (schematic).

With this example we have explored different pathways opened up by a method now used in zoology, in order to shed light on the past history of bird sounds. We must compare: the songs of different species, the calls of different species, the calls and song of a given species, the various calls of a given species. If we encounter similarities, then we must examine how great the probability of a common origin is. The degree of correspondence can be checked by experimental studies—a possibility which is not open to us when exploring movement patterns in this connection. Now and then, as is the case in comparative anatomy, two completely different structures can be related to each other—so long as we have an unbroken chain of intermediate forms. The juvenile development of a call can bring such connections to light.

Using a bit of caution, we can generally say this much right now: the alarm calls and rivalry calls of a species are frequently related to each other and to song. With regard to song, closely related species usually agree only in principle. With regard to calls, the qualitative agreement is occasionally very good. Further investigations will show whether these statements do, in fact, represent general rules or merely special instances.

XII. *Sound Parasitism*

For a long time people debated to what other avian group the viduines were most closely related. The improbable and close correspondence in palate markings, bill papillae, and plumage coloring led ornithologists to regard the viduines and the grassfinches as close relatives. But that is certainly wrong, as studies by Nicolai (1964) and Steiner (1965) have shown. The common features of the two groups are based on other causes. Female vidu-

Fɪɢ. 83.   With the nest-lure call of the host species, a male shaft-tailed whydah (*Tretaenura regia*) calls the attention of a female shaft-tailed whydah to a male of the host species who is building his nest. (After Nicolai, 1964.)

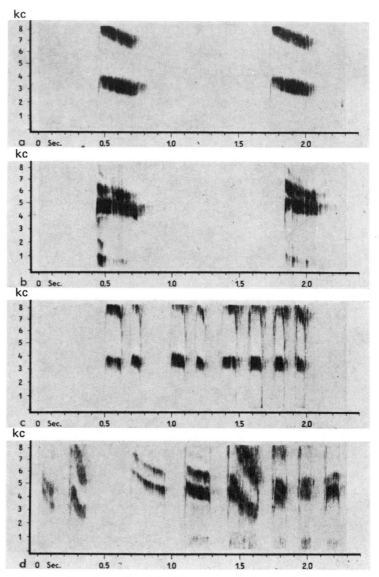

Fig. 84. Location call and food-begging call of a host bird orange-winged pytilia (*Pytilia afra*) and of a parasitic broad-tailed paradise whydah (*Steganur obtusa*): (*a*, *b*) location calls, (*c*, *d*) food-begging calls, (*a*, *c*) host bird, (*b*, *d*) brood parasite. (After Nicolai, 1964.)

ines lay their eggs in the nests of specific grassfinch species
(Fig. 83) and give no further attention to their brood. It
is the host parents who take over the task of raising both
their own youngsters and the parasitic aliens.

Now the grassfinches do not feed nestlings who differ
from their own young. If any of the youngsters evince differences, they will end up dead. But the small nest para-

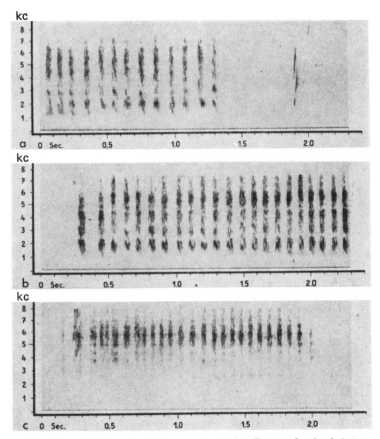

Fig. 85.   Chatter of viduine species: (*a*) village indigobird (*Hy-
pochera chalybeata*), (*b*) red-billed village indigobird (*vidua
chalybeata amauropteryx*), (*c*) shaft-tailed whydah (*Tretaenura
regia*). (After Nicolai, 1964.)

sites must not only look like their stepbrothers and sisters; they must also show a command of the begging motions which are unique among songbirds. Just hatched chicks will turn their occiput 90 to 160 degrees to the nest floor until their open beak juts outward and upward. That is one of the releasers which prompt the parents to pump food into the young chick's beak. Other releasers are the begging call and the location call. These, too, are closely adapted to those of the host bird's young (Fig. 84).

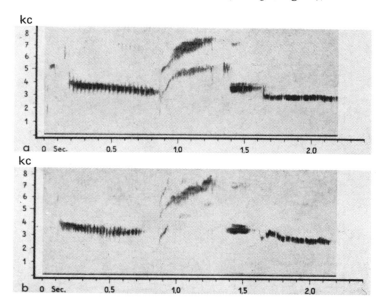

FIG. 86. (*a*) Portion of the song of the melba finch. (*b*) 'Imitation' of this song by a acacia paradise whydah. (After Nicolai, 1964.)

But the vocalizations of the host bird take a far stronger hold on the brood parasites. All viduine species sing a very similar chatter strophe (Fig. 85) when two males are fighting. Other strophes are peculiar to each viduine species. If a female is in the vicinity, males will prefer to emit the latter song. The strophes addressed to the female are perfect 'imitations' of the vocalizations of the host species (Fig. 86).

There are two possible explanations for this. Either the viduines, both male and female, learn the strophes from their foster parents—the only difference being that the males also produce them on their own; or else the vocal similarity with the host species is fixed by heredity just as the morphological adaptations are. Here something alien to the species brings about the mating and synchronization of the sexes. This is possible because a viduine species always parasitizes only one grassfinch species and closely matches all the geographic variations of the song of its host species.

If the host species happens to split up into two species, the viduine species follows suit. Nicolai made this discovery, which astonished even zoologists who are used to all kinds of things. Having made this discovery, he was able to determine the host of a viduine species from the vocalizations of the male viduine alone—insofar as the vocalizations of the host species were known to him. The follow-up verification confirmed his diagnosis in every case.

XIII. *Juvenile Development*

a) *A bird grows up*

Some calls uttered by a young bird for the first time in its life are already complete and perfect, even when they appear as early as the age of fifteen days. Others develop slowly into their definitive form, which is more or less stereotyped.

Very soon after hatching, our two treecreeper species utter a simple 'hip' call, which is repeated without variation at first (Fig. 87). It tells the parents that their offspring are hungry. On the fifth or sixth day of life, this call changes somewhat; but the change can only be seen on the sound spectrogram. Now the components of each call, which drop in pitch, are more pronounced. By the eighth day the 'primitive' calls disappear almost completely. Around the ninth or tenth day the calls of the young treecreeper are more and more prolonged. For the first time we see zigzag lines on the spectrogram; they result from rapid alterations in pitch. The pitch range is narrowed at the same time. In the third week of life the calls have pretty much assumed their definitive form, as is evident from a comparison with the corresponding calls of adult birds in the wild.

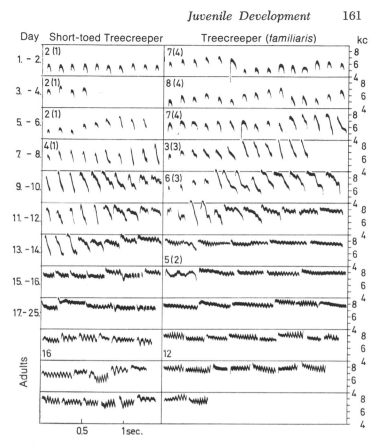

FIG. 87. Development of the begging call from the first day of life to the adult sound-contact call. The pauses between the calls do not correspond to the normal intervals. Numbers not in parentheses above the spectrographic pictures indicate the number of individuals studied. Numbers in parentheses indicate the number of the brood to which the individuals belonged.

Once the young treecreepers have become self-reliant around the fourth to sixth week, they no longer need their begging call. Now they must hunt for their own food. Yet the treecreepers do not give up this call; they retain it permanently. The only thing that changes is its meaning. Henceforth it will serve as a sound-contact call, because treecreepers do not like to be alone at any time during the year. As their name suggests, they hop up trees. In so doing they can easily lose sight of their companions. When that happens, they emit a 'srih' call which develops at some point from their childhood begging call. During the breeding period, they revert back to their childhood. They happily go back to youthful behavior patterns for the rituals of breeding preparation and pair maintenance. The female flutters her wings like a hungry chick and calls 'srih' at short intervals. Thereupon the male feeds his mate (see chapter 8, section i).

In the early youth of many oscines, one will detect a soft, monotonous twitter. It soon becomes more varied. In the fall, the first elements or motifs show up. They will also be in evidence later, and in the spring they will grow louder, clearer, and more frequent. Apart from the motifs, which were echoed by our blackbird when they were played to it at a very early age, a hint of the first learned elements shows up in September—but only singly or in twos at first (Fig. 88). In December the blackbird sang the first four elements as a group for the first time. It took more time for the bird to join all six elements together and attune them closely to the original he had heard earlier. The first learned motifs show up before the song becomes louder.

In the period when the song becomes louder, the blackbird can do a split-second switch from soft twittering to loud song motifs. The 'quality' of the song is correspondingly unstable and variable. In soft song the elements are more variable, and they are interspersed with juvenile twittering. The British aptly refer to the process of song development as 'crystallization'.

b) 'Artificial' song

Using an artificial technique, we can induce birds to sing at a very early age. All we have to do is to treat them with the male sex hormone, injecting small doses into the

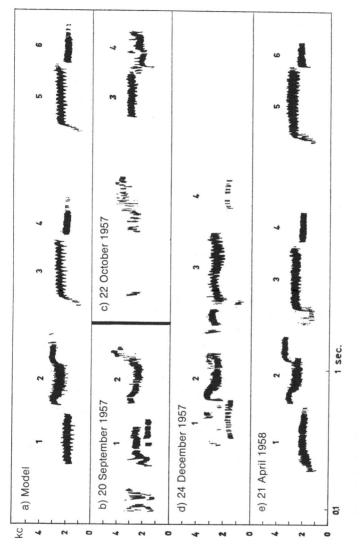

Fig. 88. (a) Blackbird strophe which was played in June to a blackbird chick born in May. (b, c) The first motifs of the young blackbird coinciding with the model, in September and October. (d) Elements 1, 2, 3, and 4 are sung together for the first time. (e) Its best agreement with the model comes during the following spring.

163

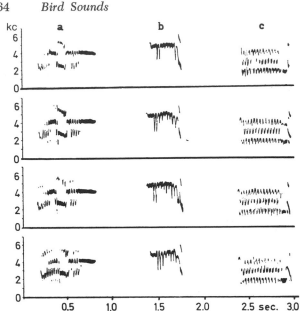

FIG. 89.   Crowing of three turkey cockerels (*a, b, c*) that were induced to sing at the age of from seven to ten days by testosterone injections. (After Marler, Kreith, and Willis, 1962.)

pectoral muscles or under the skin. Using this procedure, one can induce crowing in young turkey cockerels at the age of 8–10 days (Marler and co-workers, 1962). Each male soon develops a consistent crowing by which he can be recognized individually (Fig. 89). At this early age the crowing sounds like squealing. If we dispense more testosterone to the same birds 14–30 days later, the crowing sounds much more natural. The difference is demonstrable on spectrograms (Fig. 90). At three to five weeks of age, the crowing is longer and lower, the pitch range is narrower, and the overtones are now louder. The rapid variations in pitch, recognizable as zigzag lines on the spectrogram, no longer extend over such a wide pitch range.

In the case of the blackbird too, we found that hormone treatment produced differences in song formation which varied with the bird's age. After hormone treatments six-weeks-old blackbirds sang as loud as untreated blackbirds do the following spring; but their elements are impure, and the learned portions are not true to the model pattern. We can only pinpoint them for sure at an age when learned elements also show up in untreated birds.

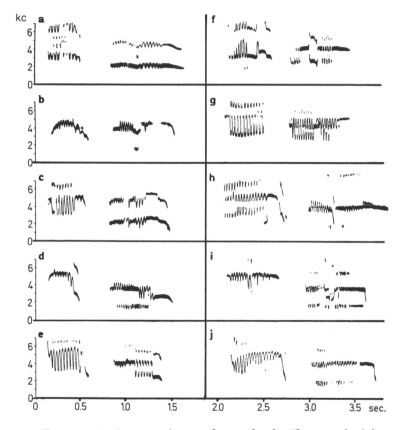

FIG. 90 *a–j.* Crowing of ten turkey cockerels. Those on the left were about one week old. Those on the right were about three to five weeks old. (After Marler, Kreith, and Willis, 1962.)

Thus cockerels and blackbirds can sing very loudly at quite an early age, but their song is imperfect in other respects. Furthermore, even at this early age the sense organs of the blackbird are transmitting complex sound impressions. The brain stores up this information long before the executive organs of the body reproduce what has been heard without the aid of artificial hormone treatment. We do not know whether the reason lies in the not yet fully developed vocal apparatus or in the nervous system.

c) *Deaf birds*

Even if turkey cockerels are deafened on their first day of life, they will crow later on just like hearing cockerels do; and all their calls will develop quite normally. They do not require any acoustic self-control for this. Even different shadings of a given call, geared as appropriate responses to outside stimuli of varying intensity, are completely normal in deaf birds.

With young oscines the course of development is different. It has been studied most thoroughly in chaffinches (Nottebohm, 1967). Earlier illustrations (Figs. 48 and 54) have already acquainted us with a normal chaffinch strophe. When male chaffinches were deafened at the age of 3–4 months, they produced very imperfect song the next spring (Fig. 91). One of the three could only emit a continuous screech (91 C). And the others had very atypical, noise-like elements that were hazily structured (91 A and B). Before being deafened, both had merely twittered in a 'primitive' way; their song was equivalent to the earliest stage of juvenile song.

When chaffinches were deafened in their first winter, they sang strophes composed of simple elements that were quite uniform and monotonous (Fig. 92). Only one (92 C) of four males was inclined to divide his strophes into phrases.

In their first spring two males sang loudly, one for one day and the other for two or more days, but not with any

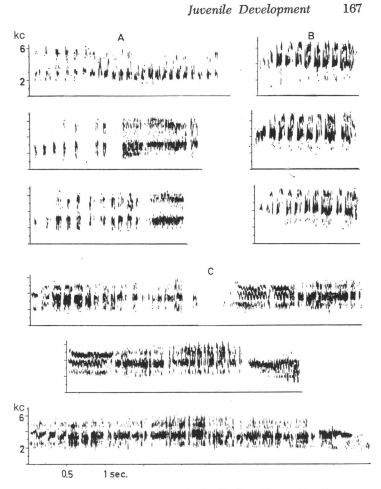

Fig. 91. Strophes of three male chaffinches (*A, B, C*) who were deafened at the age of three to four months. (After Nottebohm, 1967.)

stereotyped strophes. They were then deafened. The male who had longer practice in loud singing was the one who divided his strophes most clearly into phrases after being deafened. This tendency was weak in the other two. None of them sang an end flourish.

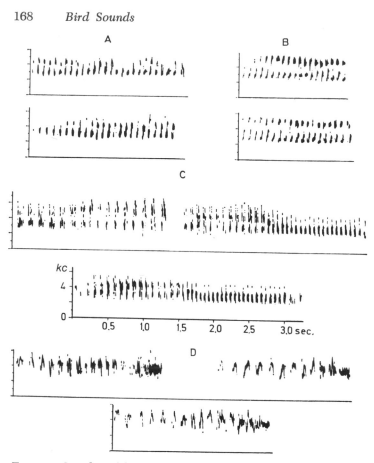

FIG. 92.   Strophes of four male chaffinches (*A, B, C, D*) who were deafened in their first winter. (After Nottebohm, 1967.)

For twelve days one male 'tested' a loud 'plastic' song. Occasionally during this period he sang almost complete and perfect strophes (Fig. 93 a). Then he was deafened. His song 'deteriorated': the elements became less consistent, and the phrases became unnaturally long (Fig. 93 b, c, d, e).

Nottebohm waited and deafened four males in the winter after their first breeding period. These birds had already been singing stereotyped strophes for several months. Their strophes did not change the next spring and summer. They no longer needed any acoustic self-control.

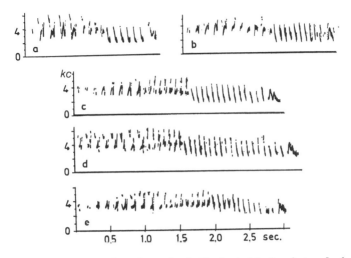

FIG. 93. Five strophes of a male chaffinch: (*a*) before being deafened (16 February 1966), (*b–e*) after being deafened. (*b*) (1 April 1966), (*c*) (6 April 1966), (*d*) (13 April 1966), (*e*) (19 April 1966). (After Nottebohm, 1967.)

The results of Nottebohm's experiments can be summarized as follows. The shorter the normal period of individual song practice, the more imperfect chaffinch song is. As long as the song remains plastic in the first spring, the bird must be able to hear itself. Otherwise deterioration will take place, even if the strophes are almost fully developed.

From studies of innate and learned factors we already know that some birds retain what they have heard in early youth and can reproduce it themselves the next spring. Now we can add another piece of information. This 'knowledge', which has been stored in the brain, must be produced for a certain length of time by the individual bird before it can be reproduced faultlessly without any acoustic self-control.

Other song birds are capable of developing their juvenile song somewhat further, even when they have been deafened. Closely related species, such as the Oregon junco and the Mexican junco (Konishi, 1964), can differ fundamentally in this respect. None of the oscine species studied so far have developed fully normal song as turkey cockerels do.

XIV. *The Yearly Cycle*

Birds do not sing and call an equal amount throughout the year. Anyone with an ear for bird sounds knows that. In our region only a few species sing in the winter. Now and then one can hear a wren or a robin singing. The influence of the weather is a drastic one at that time of year. The wind and the cold have a very deleterious effect on the frequency of avian song.

Toward spring song becomes more and more frequent. For a long time we have known that the progress of song parallels the growth of the testes, and numerous studies have shown which hormone triggers song. It is the male sex hormone, testosterone, whose effect has already been described (chapter 13, section b). English robins reach their song maximum as early as February. English song thrushes and blue tits reach it in March. Chaffinches and blackbirds do not reach it until May (Cox, 1944). Most species are very quite during the August molt. Many species reach a song peak once again in the fall, e.g., the starling, the chiffchaff, and the black redstart. Here again we can ascertain gonadal activity.

If we take birds in captivity and offer them an increasing amount of daylight after the shortened day of late fall,

Green woodpecker

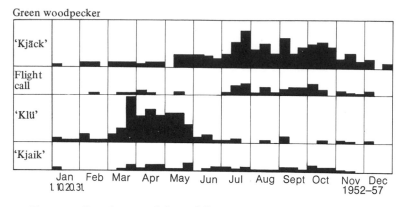

FIG. 94.   Distribution of three different calls and the song ('klü') of the green woodpecker in the course of the year. (After Blume, 1961, altered.)

we get full song from them in mid-November. Even under natural conditions not all the sounds of a given species reach their maximum in the spring. Consider the four vocal sounds of the green woodpecker, for example. Only the 'klü' song reaches its peak from March to May (Fig. 94). The 'kjäck' call is heard mainly from July to October when they are guiding the young and settling down in new quarters. The frequency of the threatening call 'kjaik' is different again, being heard throughout the year with about equal frequency (Blume, 1961).

Seasonal fluctuations affect not only the quantity of song but also its quality. We can observe this in blackbirds and chaffinches during the early spring. It is evident not only in young males but also in adult males. To a certain extent the latter repeat the process of song development each year, shifting from soft juvenile twittering to loud adult motifs.

XV. *The Daily Cycle*

Seasonal variation in song frequency is matched by similar variation over the course of the day. In general we can note a song peak in the early morning and in the evening. White wagtails in Egypt have a song maximum only at daybreak during spring. In the fall, by contrast, they sing most from late morning to noon (Hartley, 1946). Willingness to sing is influenced by temperature, winds, and cloud coverage, by the brooding phase and inner readiness. Armstrong (1963) treats this subject in detail.

The start of song in the morning differs from species to species, and it varies during the course of the year. Since we can determine precisely when avian song activity starts and finishes in the wild, bird sounds helped to serve as the foundation for a model of daily activity among wild animals (Aschoff and Wever, 1962).

XVI. *Bird Sounds and Music*

Much has been written about this topic. Indeed there is a whole book dealing with the music in the song of an avian species. It contributes only little to the subject because, in my opinion, we still know very little about bird sounds or about music.

Before we compare bird sounds and music, we must ask ourselves how competent experts define human music. Here is one definition (Riemann, 1967): "Where this term applies—in the West—music is the artistic shaping of resonant sound which, as nature and emotional call, signifies the world and the psyche with conceptual concreteness in the realm of hearing and which, as art, spiritualizes this signification and gives it expression by means of a materiality that has been reflected upon and ordered by theory and that is therefore meaningful and meaning-fashioning in itself."

Up to now we can only state that birds do have at their disposal some of the basic elements which are also components of music. For example, they transpose into different pitches, transform various imperfect melodies into

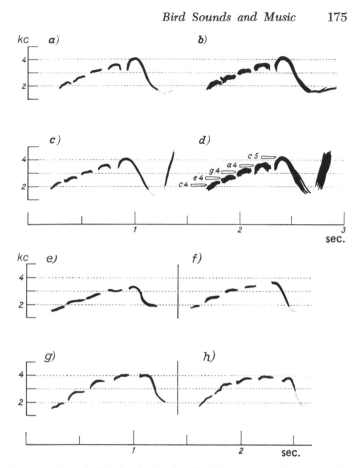

Fig. 95.   (*a, c*) Shepherd whistle, (*b, d*) imitations by a crested lark. Six (*b*) and ten (*d*) imitations imposed on one another indicate the narrow range of variation. Piano tones are indicated before the elements in (*d*). (*e, f, g, h*) Four whistle sequences of the shepherd indicate their wide range of variation. (After Tretzel, 1965 b, altered.)

clean ones, or at the very least imitate the rare clean melody amid a host of imperfect ones (Fig. 95). One striking example is the regular succession of certain strophes emitted by the American wood pewee.

XVII. *Conclusion*

Our knowledge of the various topics treated in this book is as varied and heterogeneous as the different disciplines that have some connection with bioacoustics. Much is pretty well certain already; but often we lack descriptions of the basic facts, that is, the very foundation for any research.

As a branch of comparative behavioral research, sound study has been profoundly influenced by that discipline. This is evident in the scope and range of various sections, e.g., our treatment of learning. Much work remains to be done before we have a well-rounded knowledge of bioacoustics in all its aspects.

Bibliography

Armstrong, E. A. 1963. *A study of bird song*. New York and Toronto: Oxford University Press.

Aschoff, J., and Wever, R. 1962. Beginn und Ende der täglichen Aktivität freilebender Vögel. *J. Orn.* 103: 2–27.

Bandorf, H. 1968. Beiträge zum Verhalten des Zwergtauchers (*Podiceps ruficollis*). *Vogelwelt* Beiheft 1: 7–61.

Bauer, K. M., and Glutz von Blotzheim, U. N. 1966. *Handbuch der Vögel Mitteleuropas*. Band 1. Frankfurt.

Berck, K. H. 1961. Beiträge zur Ethologie des Feldsperlings (*Passer montanus*) und dessen Beziehung zum Haussperling (*Passer domesticus*). *Vogelwelt* 82: 129–72; 83: 8–26.

Berndt, R., and Meise, W. 1959. *Naturgeschichte der Vögel*. Stuttgart.

Blase, B. 1960. Die Lautäusserungen des Neuntöters (*Lanius c. collurio* L.): Freilandbeobachtungen und Kaspar-Hauser-Versuche. *Z. Tierpsych.* 17: 293–344.

Blume, D. 1961. Über die Lebensweise einiger Spechtarten (*Dendrocopus major, Picus viridis, Dryocopus martius*). *J. Orn.* 102. Sonderheft.

177

Bremond, J. 1968. Recherches sur la semantique et les elements vecteurs d'information dans les signaux acoustiques du Rouge-Rorge (*Erithecus rubecula* L.) *La Terre et la Vie* 2: 109–220.

Brockway, Barbara F. 1962. The effects of nest-entrance positions and male vocalizations on reproduction in budgerigars. *Living Bird* 1: 93–101.

—— 1965. Stimulation of ovarian development and egg laying by male courtship vocalization in budgerigars (*Melopsittacus undulatus*). *Animal Behav.* 13: 575–78.

Chamberlain, D. R., Gross, W. B., Cornwell, G. W., and Mosby, H. S. 1968. Syringeal anatomy in the common crow. *Auk* 85: 244–52.

Conrads, K. 1966. Der Egge-Dialekt des Buchfinken (Fringilla coelebs): Ein Beitrag zur geographischen Gesangsvariation. *Vogelwelt* 87: 176–82.

Cox, P. R. 1944. A statistical investigation into bird-song. *British Birds* 38: 3–9.

Curio, E. 1959. Verhaltensstudien am Trauerschnäpper. *Z. Tierpsych.* Beiheft 3.

—— 1963. Probleme des Feinderkennens bei Vögeln. *Proc.* XIII Internat. Ornith. Congress. 1963, 206–39.

Deckert, G. 1962. Zur Ethologie des Feldsperlings (*Passer m. montanus* L.). *J. Orn.* 103: 428–86.

Dobzhansky, Th., and Pavlovsky, O. 1957. An experimental study of interaction between genetic drift and natural selection. *Evolution* 11: 311–19.

Goethe, F. 1955. Beobachtungen bei der Aufzucht junger Silbermöwen. *Z Tierpsych.* 12: 402–33.

Gompertz, T. 1967. The hiss-display of the great tit (*Parus major*). *Vogelwelt* 88: 165–69.

—— 1968. Results of bringing individuals of two geographically isolated forms of *Parus major* into contact. *Vogelwelt* Beiheft 1: 63–92.

Goodwin, D. 1967. *Pigeons and doves of the world.* Trustees of the British Museum (Natural History).

Gwinner, E., and Kneutgen, J. 1962. Über die biologische Bedeutung der 'zweckdienlichen' Anwendung erlernter Laute bei Vögeln. Z. *Tierpsych.* 19: 692–96.

Haartman, L. V. 1953. Was reizt den Trauerfliegenschnäpper (*Muscicapa hypoleuca*) zu füttern? *Vogelwelt* 16: 157–64.

Hamilton III, W. J. 1962. Evidence concerning the function of nocturnal call notes of migratory birds. *Condor* 64: 390–401.

Harrison, C. J. O. 1962. Solitary song and its inhibition in some estrildidae. *J. Orn.* 103: 369–79.

Hartley, P. H. T. 1946. The song of the white wagtail in winter quarters. *British Birds* 39: 44–47.

Iljitschew, W. D., and Iswekowa, L. M. 1963. in W. D. Iljitschew, Die Mauser der Ohrfedern. *Falke* 14: 202–3.

Immelmann, K. 1962. Beiträge zu einer vergleichenden Biologie australischer Prachtfinken (Spermestidae). *Zool. Jb. Syst.* 90: 1–196.

——— 1967. Zur ontogenetischen Gesangsentwicklung bei Prachtfinken. Verh. Deutsch. Zool. Ges. Göttingen 1966, *Zool. Anz.* 30, Supplement, 320–32.

Kirby, J., Brown, Ph., and Zweers, K. *So singen die Vögel.* No. 8 (record title).

Koehler, O. 1951. Der Vogelgesang als Vorstufe für Musik und Sprache. *J. Orn.* 93: 3–20.

Konishi, M. 1964. Song variation in a population of Oregon juncos. *Condor* 66: 423–36.

Kuhk, R. 1966. Aus der Sinneswelt des Rauhfusskauzes (*Aegolius funereus*). *Anz. orn. Ges. Bayern* 7: 714–16.

Löhrl, II. 1955. Schlafgewohnheiten der Baumläufer (*Certhia brachydactyla, Certhia familiaris*) und anderer Kleinvögel in kalten Winternächten. *Vogelwarte* 18: 71–77.

——— 1959. Zur Frage des Zeitpunktes einer Prägung auf die Heimatregion beim Halsbandschnäpper (*Ficedula albicollis*). *J. Orn.* 100: 132–40.

—— 1968. *Tiere und wir*. Frankfurt, Berlin, and Vienna.

Lorenz, K. 1935. Der Kumpan in der Umwelt des Vogels. *J. Orn.* 83: 137–213, 289–413.

Lott, D., Scholz, Susan D., and Lehrman, D. S. 1967. Exteroceptive stimulation of the reproductive system of the female ring dove (*Streptopelia risoria*) by the mate and by the colony milieu. *Animal Behaviour* 15: 433–37.

Marler, P. 1956. Über die Eigenschaften einiger tierlicher Rufe. *J. Orn.* 97: 220–27.

—— 1957. Specific distinctiveness in the communication signals of birds. *Behaviour* 11: 13–39.

—— 1967. Comparative study of song development in sparrows. *Proc.* XIV Intern. Ornith. Congr., 1966, 231–44.

Marler, P., Kreith, M., and Willis, E. 1962. An analysis of testosterone-induced crowing in young domestic cockerels. *Animal Behaviour* 10: 48–54.

Marler, P., Tamura, M. 1964. Culturally transmitted patterns of vocal behaviour in sparrows. *Science* 146: 1483–86.

Mayr, E. 1963. *Animal species and evolution*. Cambridge, Massachusetts.

Meise, W. 1928. Die Verbreitung der Aaskrähe (Formenkreis *Corvus corone* L.). *J. Orn.* 76: 1–203.

Messmer, E., and Messmer, I. 1956. Die Entwicklung der Lautäusserungen und einiger Verhaltensweisen der Amsel (*Turdus merula* L.) unter natürlichen Bedingungen und nach Einzelaufenthalt in schalldichten Räumen. *Z. Tierpsych.* 13: 341–441.

Moynihan, M., and Hall, M. F. 1954. Hostile sexual and other social behaviour patterns of the spice finch (*Lonchura punctulata*) in captivity. *Behaviour* 7: 33–76.

Mulligan, J. A. 1966. Singing behaviour and its development in the song sparrow (*Melospita melodia*). *Univ. Calif. Public. Zool.* 81: 1–76.

Nicolai, J. 1959. Familientradition in der Gesangsentwicklung des Gimpels (*Pyrrhula pyrrhula* L.). *J. Orn.* 100: 39–46.

—— 1962. Comments on Harrison's work (1962, see above) in *J. Orn.* 103: 369–79.

—— 1964. Der Brutparasitismus der Viduinae als ethologisches Problem. *Z. Tierpsych.* 21: 129–204.

Niethammer, G. 1937. *Handbuch der deutschen Vogelkunde.* Bd. 1, Leipzig.

Nottebohm, F. 1967. The role of sensory feedback in the development of avian vocalizations. *Proc.* XIV Intern. Ornith. Congress, 265–80.

Payne, R. S. 1962. How the barn owl locates prey by hearing. *Living Bird* 1: 151–59.

Poulsen, H. 1951. Inheritance and learning in the song of the chaffinch (*Fringilla coelebs* L.). *Behaviour* 3: 216–28.

Reinig, W. F. 1938. *Elimination und Selektion.* Jena.

Remane, A. 1952. *Die Grundlagen des natürlichen Systems der vergleichenden Anatomie und der Phylogenetik.* Leipzig.

Riemann, H. 1967. *Musiklexikon.* Mainz.

Rüppell, W. 1933. Physiologie und Akustik der Vogelstimme. *J. Orn.* 81: 433–542.

Rutschke, E. 1966. Über den Bau and die Färbung der Vogelfeder. *Falke* 13: 292–99.

Sauer, F. 1954. Die Entwicklung der Lautäusserungen vom Ei ab schalldicht gehaltener Dorngrasmücken (*Sylvia c. communis* Latham). *Z. Tierpsych.* 11: 1–93.

Schleidt, W. M. 1964. Über die Spontaneität von Erbkoordinationen. *Z. Tierpsych.* 21: 235–56.

Schleidt, W. M., Schleidt, M., and Magg, M. 1960. Störung der Mutter-Kind-Beziehung bei Truthühnern durch Gehörverlust. *Behaviour* 16: 254–60.

Schwartzkopff, J. 1955. Schallsinnesorgane: ihre Funktion und biologische Bedeutung bei Vögeln. *Acta* XI Congr. Intern. Ornith. 1954.

—— 1960. Vergleichende Physiologie des Gehörs. *Fortschritte Zoologie*. 12: 206–64.

—— 1965. Die Verarbeitung von Sinnesnachrichten im Organismus. *Festschrift* Eröffn. Univ. Bochum: F. Kamp, Bochum.

Sheldon, W. G. 1967. *The book of the american woodcock.* Amherst: University Massachusetts.

Sick, H. 1959. Die Balz der Schmuckvögel (*Pipridae*). *J. Orn.* 100: 269–302.

Simmons, K. E. L. 1955. The nature of predator-reactions of waders toward humans: with special reference to the role of the aggressive, escape, and brooding drives. *Behaviour* 8: 130–73.

Smith, N. G. 1966. Evolution of some arctic gulls (*Larus*): an experimental study of isolating mechanisms. *Ornithological Monographs,* Number 4.

Stein, R. C. 1968. Modulation in bird sounds. *Auk* 85: 229–43.

Steiner, H. 1965. Der Brutparasitismus der Viduinae: ein eigenartiger Fall echter Mimikry. *Zool. Jb. System* 92: 167–82.

Stresemann, E. 1919. Über die europäischen Baumläufer. *Verh. Orn. Ges. Bayern* 14: 39–74.

—— 1927–34. Aves. In Kükenthal-Krumbach, *Handb. Zool.* 7; 2nd half, Berlin and Leipzig.

Thielcke, G. 1970. Die sozialen Funktionen der Vogelstimmen. *Vogelwarte* 25: 204–229.

Thielcke, H., and Thielcke, G. 1960. Akustisches Lernen verschieden alter schallisolierter Amseln (*Turdus merula* L.) und die Entwicklung erlernter Motive ohne und mit künstlichem Einfluss von Testosteron. *Z. Tierpsych.* 17: 211–44.

Thorpe, W. H. 1954. The process of song-learning in the chaffinch as studied by means of the sound spectrograph. *Nature* 173: 465–75.

—— 1958. The learning of song patterns by birds: with

special reference to the song of the chaffinch (*Fringilla coelebs*). *Ibis*. 100: 535–70.

—— 1961. *Bird song*. Cambridge.

Todt, D. 1968. Wiederholung akustischer Muster im Gesang der Amsel. *Naturw*. 55: 450.

Tretzel, E. 1965. Über das Spotten der Singvögel, insbesondere ihre Fähigkeit zu spontaner Nachahmung. Verh. Deutsch. Zool. Ges. Kiel 1964, *Zool. Anz.*, Suppl. 28: 556–65.

—— 1965. Imitation und Variation von Schäferpfiffen durch Haubenlerchen (*Galerida c. cristata* L.): Ein Beispiel für spezielle Spottmotiv-Prädisposition. *Z. Tierpsych*. 22: 784–809.

—— 1967. Spottmotivprädisposition und akustische Abstraktion bein Gartengrasmücken (Sylvia borin borin/ Bodd./). Verh. Deutsch. Zool. Ges., Göttingen, 1966, *Zool. Anz.* Suppl. 30: 333–43.

Tschanz, B. 1968. Trottellummen. *Z. Tierpsych*. Beiheft 4.

Veprinstev, B. N., and Naoomova, Z. R. 1964. *The voices of wild nature: siberian birds*. Record.

Vince, M. A. 1964. Social facilitation of hatching in the bobwhite quail. *Animal Behaviour* 12: 531–34.

—— 1966. Artificial acceleration of hatching in quail embryos. *Animal Behaviour* 14: 389–94.

—— 1967. Wie synchronisieren Wachteljunge im Ei den Schlüpftermin? *Umschau*. 415–19.

—— 1968. Effect of rate of stimulation on hatching time in japanese quail. *Brit. Poultry Science* 9: 87–91.

Wall, W. von de 1963. Bewegungsstudien an Anatiden. *J. Orn*. 104: 1–15.

Weeden, J. S., and Falls, J. B. 1959. Differential responses of male ovenbirds to recorded songs of neighboring and more distant individuals. *Auk* 76: 343–51.

Picture Credits

Illustrations taken from other authors are indicated in the preceding bibliography, where the source work is cited. All the rest are original, except for the few which come from other articles and which are cited below:

Figure 2: Die Auswertung von Vogelstimmen nach Tonbandaufnahmen. *Vogelwelt* 87: 1–14.

Figure 26: Zur Phylogenese einiger Lautäusserungen der europäischen Baumläufer. *Z. zool. Syst. Evolutionsforsch.* 2: 383–413.

Figure 27: Zur geographischen Variation des Gesanges des Zilpzalps in Mittel- und Südwesteuropa mit einem Vergleich des Gesanges des Fitis. *J. Orn.* 104: 372–402.

Figure 28: Die sozialen Funktionen verschiedener Gesangsformen des Sonnenvogels. *Z. Tierpsych.* 27: 177–85.

Figures 29, 52, 89: Ergebnisse der Vogelstimmen-Analyse. *J. Orn.* 102: 285–300.

Figures 53, 55, 56, 57, 58, 71, 72: Geographic variation in bird vocalizations. In Hinde, *Bird vocalizations.* Cambridge, 1969.

Figures 59, 64: Gesangsgeographische Variation des Gartenbaumläufers im Hinblick auf das Artbildungsproblem. Z. *Tierpsych.* 22: 542–66.

Figures 68, 70, 76: Entstehung neuer Tierarten. *Sandorama.* December, 1965.

Figure 75: Die Reaktion von Tannen- und Kohlmeise auf den Gesang nahverwandter Formen. *J. Orn.* 110: 148–57.

Figures 78, 79: Gemeinsames der Gattung *Parus:* Ein bioakustischer Beitrag zur Systematik. *Vogelwelt* Beiheft 1: 147–64.

Figure 88: Die Ontogenese der Bettellaute von Garte-nund Waldbaumläufer. *Zool. Anz.* 174: 237–41.

Index of Species Cited